WHEN THE CHIPS ARE DOWN

When the Chips Are Down

Problem Gambling in America

Rachel A. Volberg

A Century Foundation Report

2001 • The Century Foundation Press • New York

The Century Foundation sponsors and supervises timely analyses of economic policy, foreign affairs, and domestic political issues. Not-for-profit and nonpartisan, it was founded in 1919 and endowed by Edward A. Filene.

LIBRARY OF CONGRESS CATALOGING-IN-PUBLICATION DATA
Volberg, Rachel A., 1954–
    When the chips are down : problem gambling in America / by Rachel A. Volberg.
        p. cm. — (A century foundation report)
    Includes bibliographical references and index.
    ISBN 0-87078-469-2 (pbk.)
    1. Gambling—United States. 2. Gamblers—United States. 3. Compulsive gamblers—United States. 4. Compulsive gambling—United States. I. Title. II. Series.
    HV6715 .V76 2001
    362.2'5—dc21

                                                                2001002827

Cover Design and illustration by Claude Goodwin
Manufactured in the United States of America.

In memoriam

Anselm Strauss—"study the unstudied"

FOREWORD

The 1999 report of the National Gambling Impact Study Commission, the most comprehensive look at gambling in the United States to date, makes clear one dramatic change that has taken place in America since the mid-1970s: We have gone from a nation in which legal gambling activity was extremely rare—casinos in only one state, a handful of state lotteries, and fairly common, but small-scale, pari-mutuel activities—to a nation in which legal gambling, in one form or another, is permitted in all but three states. Today, tens of millions of citizens engage in some form of legal gambling every day.

Not only has commercial gambling become an immense industry, but state and local governments are heavily involved in the active pursuit of gambling revenues, either directly through lotteries and similar government-operated gambling or through taxes and permit fees for commercial gambling. And another category of governments—tribal nations—has emerged as a leader in the spread of gambling throughout the nation. Yet, despite the enormous growth of legalized gambling, there has been remarkably little serious research about its effects. The casino industry does support limited research, but, sadly, it has taken a long time to get gambling on the radar screen of the major federal funders of research on addictive behaviors. And the states, despite their expensive advocacy of lotteries, by and large are not doing much.

Those who defend the growth of gambling argue that, in fact, we do know many important things about the impact of legalization. It is, they claim, good for the economy. It legitimizes activity that, in the past, had been underground. They also argue that, for responsible adults, the decision to gamble is a reasonable choice about how to spend recreation dollars. A more philosophical justification often is constructed around the contention that the growth of gambling reflects no more than a democratic impulse expressed in referenda, by state legislatures, and through other political means.

We also know, however, that some gamblers develop patterns of behavior that are destructive both to themselves and their families. And, we know that gambling abuse is highly correlated with other pathologies. Although the more responsible members of the gambling industry acknowledge that there are those who cannot handle the temptations of gambling, the industry's basic position is that problem gamblers are a small minority who can be addressed best by targeted treatment and prevention programs. Some recent research, however, indicates that the number of problem and pathological gamblers in America is growing—a perhaps inevitable result of the increase in opportunities to gamble in recent years. Moreover, the evidence available suggests that efforts to meet the needs of problem gamblers fall far short of what it would take to seriously address the phenomenon.

At The Century Foundation, we have begun an effort to add to the body of knowledge available about gambling's impact on the nation. We cosponsored a conference with the National Center on Addiction and Substance Abuse at Columbia University, "High Stakes: Substance Abuse and Gambling." The conference aimed at finding ways to better understand the issues involved in creating sound public policy for addressing gambling problems. It drew on the Center's knowledge of the extensive programs that have been developed to deal with other popular activities that have damaging side-effects, such as drinking alcohol and smoking tobacco.

The Century Foundation is, in addition, planning several publications in this area. This volume, by Rachel Volberg, president of Gemini Research, who has directed a number of studies of gambling and problem gambling since 1986, addresses the darker side of gambling—the number of individuals with a serious addiction to gambling, its costs to society, and the need for prevention and treatment. She says that not only are some 5.5 million Americans already problem or pathological gamblers, which can have devastating effects not only on them but on their families, but that some 15 million American adults can be considered at risk for problem gambling.

Volberg argues that gambling should be considered a public health issue and recommends steps to improve monitoring, prevention, and treatment.

A second volume, by John Lyman Mason and Michael Nelson, professors of political science at Rhodes College in Memphis, Tennessee, looks at the major reasons for the rapid proliferation of gambling in the United States. It examines the politics behind gambling at the state, tribal, and federal levels, and explores the influence of interest groups, the role of campaign contributions, and public opinion in bringing about the legalization of gambling.

In the future, we hope to look into some of the other issues surrounding gambling that require more serious attention. As an example, consider the latest growth area for gambling: the Internet. The sheer magnitude of gambling offerings already available on the web provides significant potential opportunities for people to engage in the kind of behavior that results in problem and pathological gambling. Many Americans do not mind gambling in a controlled environment, where players are protected, the games are fair, and children are excluded. However, gambling at home, whether on a computer monitor or a television screen, raises a number of serious questions such as, Are parents supposed to discourage their children from using a computer in order to shield them from online casinos? More generally, the fact that many Americans want gambling to be legal does not mean that they want it everywhere. Eighteen wheelers are legal, but they do not belong on, indeed often are banned from, residential streets.

Clearly, gambling is a public policy issue in need of serious research and serious debate, and we are grateful to Rachel Volberg for this thorough exploration of a critical aspect of the problem—the problem of gambling addiction.

RICHARD C. LEONE, *President*
The Century Foundation
May 2001

CONTENTS

ACKNOWLEDGMENTS

No large writing project is ever truly the effort of a single person. Over the years, I have been privileged to work, and write, with a number of remarkably intelligent and generous colleagues. Given the amount of writing I do with others, there are occasions when I cannot recall whether a specific sentence or paragraph in a particular article or report is mine or the words of others whose names appear with mine. In the present case, my name, alone, acknowledges my responsibility for any errors or lack of judgment between these covers. The fact that only my name appears should not disguise the contributions made by many others to the quality of the work and clarity of the writing.

I must begin by acknowledging my good friend Max Abbott, whose capacity for grappling with new ideas and unblinking work ethic have inspired me for over a decade. I must also acknowledge the camaraderie, fellowship, and international perspective that Sten Rönnberg and the International Gambling Research Team of Sweden—Anders Andrèn, Jakob Jonsson, Ingrid Munck, Thomas Nilsson, and Ove Svenson—have provided since we began our in-depth investigation of problem gambling in Sweden in 1996.

Since 1998, I have been privileged to work with an inspiring group of investigators at the National Opinion Research Center. Led by Dean Gerstein, this multidisciplinary, multitalented team drew me into an organization that is geographically dispersed but intellectually focused. Working with them to carry out the research program for the National Gambling Impact Study Commission, and subsequently to develop several published papers and successful grant proposals, has demonstrated to me how very productive a good division of labor can be.

I must also acknowledge Eugene Christiansen and Sebastian Sinclair of Christiansen Capital Advisers. Eugene, especially, has challenged me to think critically about concepts that gambling researchers tend to take for granted. Sebastian has opened my eyes to the rapid evolution of gambling on the Internet and its likely impacts on problem gambling.

When I first began work in the field of gambling studies, I found an intellectual home at the National Council on Problem Gambling. The members of this diverse group shared a passionate desire to change the ways that problem gamblers were understood and treated in America. I am especially indebted to the other researchers who serve the National Council—in particular, Henry Lesieur and Richard Rosenthal. Membership in the National Council opened an unusual professional path for me—there are not many sociologists who are able to support themselves entirely outside the halls of academia. That I have been able to follow such a unique path is due largely to relationships built over fifteen years with the many members of the National Council on Problem Gambling and its affiliates.

Finally, I must express my love and gratitude to my husband, Walton Lamar Moore, and our daughter, Calyx Alexandra, as well as my sisters, my brother-in-law, and my parents. I would not be where, or who, I am without your love, support, and laughter.

1

INTRODUCTION

On my first day of work at the New York State Office of Mental Health, in early May 1985, I was handed a two-page bibliography and told "this is everything that has been published about problem gambling." My interest was piqued—how could so little be known about a subject on which public dollars were already being spent? Over the succeeding years, I have run into this situation again and again—at every legislative hearing, at every conference, in every conversation, people ask questions about problem gambling for which we researchers have few, if any, answers. After sixteen years the bibliography is longer, but there are still very few places to find a broad and comprehensive view of the issues that surround the topic of problem gambling.

This report is intended to provide readers with an understanding of the challenges posed by problem gambling to policymakers and the general public. Chapter 2 begins with a description of some of the characteristics of problem gambling, as well as the impacts of this disorder on individuals and communities. Chapter 3 discusses the rapid expansion of legal gambling and the emergence of problem gambling as a recognized medical disorder. Chapter 4 describes the extent of problem gambling in the general population and in particular groups in the population as well as the relationship between problem gambling and specific gambling activities. Chapter 5 describes the public and private efforts under way at the state and national levels to address problem gambling and examines what is known about the effectiveness of these efforts. Finally, Chapter 6 discusses some of the approaches that policymakers can take to address the issue of problem gambling.

By the end, my hope is that readers will have a clearer understanding of some of the issues that surround problem gambling, that they will realize why some of our questions about problem gambling cannot yet be answered, and that they will join me and others in the field in fostering the work that is needed to monitor the impacts of this enormous natural experiment in the coming decades.

2

WHAT IS PROBLEM GAMBLING?

For most people, gambling is an enjoyable, if occasional, experience. Whether it is buying a lottery ticket, placing a bet on a horse race, going to a casino for an evening, or wagering privately with friends, most people gamble for entertainment or for social reasons and typically do not risk more than they can afford to lose. For some people, however, gambling leads to debilitating problems that also can result in harm to people close to them and to the wider community. These are the people we call "problem gamblers."[1]

When they think about problem gamblers, most people have a stereotype in mind—someone like Marty.[2] When Marty was a child, his relatives would take him to the racetrack and place bets for him. His family's social life revolved around bingo, card games with friends, and other gambling activities. After several big wins, Marty started betting heavily in high school on sports and card games. Even while winning, Marty had fights with his parents and told many lies to get out of paying back friends from whom he had borrowed money to gamble. As an adult, still gambling heavily on sports, card games, and horses, Marty borrowed more than $25,000 from several elderly relatives. He planned to pay them back when he finally won "the big one," but instead got further and further into debt with bookmakers and loan sharks. Eventually, his wife confronted him and his family agreed to pay back everything he owed if he would quit gambling. Marty took the money and paid off his debts but kept gambling. Finally, again deep in debt and desperate, Marty went to Las Vegas with $20,000 that he had taken from the company where he

worked and lost it all. Marty was eventually arrested and served time
in prison.

Until the 1990s, treatment professionals and gambling researchers as well as journalists and the general public assumed that this picture was accurate for all problem gamblers.[3] But the reality of
problem gambling is more complex and diverse than this stereotype.
While the story of Patty Van Hooser does not fit the stereotype, she
is nevertheless just as much of a problem gambler as Marty.

A single mom at the age of twenty-two, Patty worked odd jobs
and struggled to bring up two kids. Patty started getting into trouble
with her gambling when she won big on bingo, once. Within a few
years, she was gambling daily on slot machines at a local casino on
the way home from work. It was a way to escape the stress of caring
for her elderly parents, her second husband, and her troubled children. She began borrowing from friends, cashing bad checks, and
using family food money to gamble. After a suicide attempt, Patty
joined Gamblers Anonymous. She and her husband had to sell her car,
refinance their mortgage, and file for bankruptcy. But Patty's story
ends happily—she now works as an administrator for a small nonprofit group that counsels problem gamblers.[4]

DEFINING OUR TERMS

While there is general agreement that some people experience serious
problems associated with their gambling, a confusing array of terms
has been used to refer to individuals who experience such difficulties.
Some of these terms include problem gambling, excessive gambling,
disordered gambling, compulsive gambling, addictive gambling, and
pathological gambling. Debates about terminology among gambling
researchers have centered on two issues: the difficulties of comparing
data that are based on different definitions and measures of gambling problems, and the importance of developing a terminology that
represents a dynamic continuum of experiences rather than arbitrary
categories.

While *problem gambling* is the term most widely used to refer to
individuals who experience difficulties with their gambling, it has
been used in a variety of ways. In some situations, it is used to indicate all of the patterns of gambling behavior that compromise, dis-
rupt, or damage personal, family, or vocational pursuits.[5] In these

instances, problem gambling refers to a continuum of gambling-related difficulties ranging from mild to extremely severe. In other situations, such as in reporting the results of epidemiological research, the term *problem gambling* is limited to those who score in a given range on one or another of the accepted screens for problem and pathological gambling.

Problem gamblers, as well as those who score even lower on problem gambling screens (sometimes referred to as *at-risk* gamblers), are of concern because they represent much larger proportions of the population than pathological gamblers alone. Problem gamblers and at-risk gamblers are also of concern because of the possibility that their gambling-related difficulties may become more severe over time. Finally, problem and at-risk gamblers are of interest because of the likelihood that their gambling will be more easily influenced by social attitudes and public awareness.[6]

Although there are numerous historical and fictional references to gambling problems, *pathological gambling* was not widely recognized as a mental disorder until the final quarter of the twentieth century. The term was first included in the *Diagnostic and Statistical Manual* (DSM) of the American Psychiatric Association in 1980.[7] Each revision of the DSM since then (in 1987 and 1994) has seen changes in the diagnostic criteria for pathological gambling as research has improved our understanding of the disorder. Currently, the essential features of pathological gambling are:

- a continuous or periodic loss of control over gambling;

- a progression, in gambling frequency and amounts wagered, in preoccupation with gambling and in obtaining money with which to gamble; and

- ✓ a continuation of gambling despite adverse consequences.[8]

A formal diagnosis of pathological gambling is usually made by a qualified and experienced clinician following a lengthy clinical interview. To make a diagnosis of pathological gambling, the clinician must determine that the patient has met five or more of the ten diagnostic indicators associated with pathological gambling. Table 2.1 (page 6) presents the most recent diagnostic criteria for pathological gambling.

TABLE 2.1. DIAGNOSTIC CRITERIA FOR
PATHOLOGICAL GAMBLING

Persistent and recurrent maladaptive gambling behavior as indicated by five (or more) of the following:

Preoccupation	Preoccupation with reliving past gambling experiences, handicapping or planning the next venture, or thinking of ways to get money with which to gamble
Tolerance	Need to gamble with increasing amounts of money in order to achieve the desired excitement
Withdrawal	Restlessness or irritability when attempting to cut down or stop gambling
Escape	Use of gambling as a way to escape problems or to relieve dysphoric mood (for example, feelings of helplessness, guilt, anxiety, or depression)
Chasing	Return to gambling after losing money in order to get even ("chasing one's losses")
Lying	Lying to family members, therapists, or others to conceal the extent of involvement with gambling
Loss of control	Repeated unsuccessful efforts to control, cut back, or stop gambling
Illegal acts	Forgery, fraud, theft, embezzlement, or other illegal acts in order to finance gambling
Risking significant relationships	Jeopardy or loss of a significant relationship, job, or educational or career opportunity because of gambling
Bailout	Reliance on others to provide money to relieve a desperate financial situation caused by gambling

The gambling behavior is not better accounted for by a manic episode, which would otherwise prevent diagnosis.

Source: Diagnostic and Statistical Manual of Mental Disorders, 4th ed. (Washington, D.C.: American Psychiatric Association, 1994). Reprinted with permission in *Responsible Gaming Resource Guide* (Washington, D.C.: American Gaming Association, 1996), Appendix 5-1.

Although pathological gambling is classified in the DSM as a disorder of impulse control, many clinicians and researchers, as well as the media, view and treat the disorder as an addiction, similar to alcohol and substance dependence. Indeed, with the exception of "chasing" and "bailout," all of the present diagnostic criteria for pathological gambling are derived from the characteristics that define alcohol, cocaine, heroin, and other forms of drug dependence.[9] The clearest illustration of this was the inclusion of "tolerance" and "withdrawal" in the DSM criteria for pathological gambling in 1994.

In gambling surveys, individuals are generally categorized as *problem gamblers* or *probable pathological gamblers* on the basis of their responses to the questions in one of the screens developed to identify individuals with gambling-related difficulties. Use of the term *probable* distinguishes the results of prevalence surveys, where classification is generally based on a telephone interview, from a clinical diagnosis. In many prevalence surveys, a distinction also is made between "lifetime" and "current" problem and probable pathological gamblers. In general, *lifetime* problem and probable pathological gamblers are individuals who, over the course of their lifetime, have met three or more of the criteria for problem or pathological gambling. *Current* problem and probable pathological gamblers are individuals who have met these criteria in the past year (or, in a few cases, the past six months).

In spite of widespread preference for the terms "problem" and "pathological" gambling, there is a need for a more refined terminology that can distinguish people who are in these groups for different reasons. For example, there are people who do not currently gamble or have gambling problems but who did in the past—this group is important because these people may be at increased risk for future development of gambling problems. The group called "problem gamblers" includes both people who are developing more serious problems and those who are experiencing a reduction in problems. There is also probably a third group who are not moving appreciably in either direction but are maintaining some level of problematic gambling. In addition, there is value in recognizing people who indicate that they personally believe that they have a gambling problem. Such individuals might not score on a screen for problem gambling, but their willingness to acknowledge difficulties has important implications for treatment planning and public health education programs.

Compared to studies of alcohol and drugs, the gambling studies field is in its infancy and there is much that we do not know about

problem and pathological gambling. For example, pathological gambling is defined as a chronic disorder—that is, a disorder that leaves
a lifelong vulnerability that may be effectively treated and kept in
check but from which the person is never entirely free. Data from
gambling treatment programs demonstrate that problem and pathological gamblers experience relapse at about the same rate as alcohol
and substance abusers. Problem and pathological gamblers who have
gone through treatment often refer to themselves as "in recovery,"
although it is unclear whether this analogy to other addictions is
entirely appropriate. Furthermore, the very limited longitudinal
research available on problem and pathological gambling suggests
that, for some people, gambling problems may be a transient life
cycle problem rather than a chronic mental disorder.[10]

WHAT PROBLEM GAMBLING IS NOT

There are several tacit ideas that people have about problem gambling that limit our understanding of this issue, including the notions
that problem gambling only affects individuals and that problem
gambling is strictly a medical condition. Social and economic institutions with which problem gamblers' lives and those of their families
intersect are structured in ways that often ignore the larger, human
context of problem gambling. We tend to think of problem gamblers
as individuals rather than as members of families and communities—
families and communities that also are affected by gambling and
gambling-related problems. While some treatment professionals do
address the challenges faced by families of problem gamblers,[11] there
is little recognition by governments, the gambling industries, or medical institutions that problem gamblers do not exist in a vacuum. I
address this limitation in a small way in this chapter by describing
some of the impacts of problem gambling on families and communities as well as on individuals.

It is also important to understand that the public acceptance of
problem and pathological gambling as a "medical" problem is the
result of the intersection of at least two unique social and historical
developments in the United States in the final quarter of the twentieth
century: the official recognition of pathological gambling as one of
several, new disorders by the psychiatric profession and the emergence of the "third wave" of gambling legalization in the 1980s.[12]

The medical view of problem gambling fits, more or less well, into the worlds of clinics and hospitals; medical professionals; academic disciplines; gambling industries; local, state, and federal governments and their agencies; insurance and financial industries; and civil and criminal justice systems that deal with problem gamblers and their families.[13] Although the medical perspective provides people with a way to think about problem gambling, make sense of their experiences, and respond, it is important to recognize that this is not the only possible way to understand and respond to this issue.

While the view of problem gambling as a psychiatric disorder is common in the United States, researchers in other countries prefer a broader, population-based model of the difficulties arising from participation in gambling. Nearly all of these researchers are based in countries with nationalized health systems, such as Australia and Canada, that have adopted "harm reduction" approaches to social problems such as alcohol and drug abuse and, more recently, problem gambling. In relation to drug use, harm reduction has been defined as "a policy or program directed towards decreasing the adverse health, social, and economic consequences of drug use without requiring abstinence."[14] Examples of harm reduction programs include methadone and needle exchange programs, responsible drinking policies and programs, and alcohol and drug treatment programs that accept controlled use, and not just abstinence, as a viable treatment goal.

Advocates of the principles of harm reduction give priority to policies and programs that focus on specific harms, that maximize the intervention options for those dealing with people who have problems, and that treat such people as members of the community rather than marginalizing them. The harm reduction perspective gives priority to interventions that target high-risk groups, that are comprehensive in scope, and that make use of existing networks of specialists and organizations.[15]

The harm reduction perspective has implications both for social policy related to gambling and for the measurement of gambling problems in the community. For example, debates about the availability of gambling in countries like Australia and Canada are less polarized than such debates in the United States. Instead, consideration is given to restrictions on advertising, careful venue design, and education and community awareness programs.[16] In measuring gambling problems, the harm reduction perspective defines problem gambling as "gambling behavior that creates negative consequences for the gambler, others in his or her social network, or for the community." This view of problem gambling seeks to measure the impacts of problem gambling on a range of stakeholders, including government agencies, health care providers, public health agencies, community organizations, private industry, schools, employers, social service and housing agencies, transportation and justice agencies, faith communities, and families as well as individuals.[17]

THE IMPACTS OF PROBLEM GAMBLING

As the preceding discussion makes clear, the impacts of problem gambling are felt not just by individuals, but also by families, communities, and many social institutions. In this section, I present information about the impacts of problem gambling in five domains: the individual or personal, the family or interpersonal, the workplace, the financial, and the legal.

Most of what is known about the impacts of problem gambling comes from studies of people who have sought professional help for their gambling problems or from members of Gamblers Anonymous. Although this approach has been effective in identifying the extent and types of consequences experienced by some problem gamblers, the National Research Council points out that the results of these studies must be interpreted with caution because of the small, atypical samples involved.[18] Furthermore, it is widely recognized that problem gamblers in treatment are not fully representative of problem gamblers in the general population.[19] While several recent reviews have identified the impacts of problem gambling in a variety of life areas,[20] it is worth emphasizing that it is not necessary for an individual to achieve the full-blown psychiatric disorder of pathological gambling to experience problematic impacts from their gambling.

INDIVIDUAL IMPACTS

Problem gambling has a variety of impacts on the individual, ranging from physical stress reactions to severe psychiatric disorders. Based on individuals in treatment, pathological gamblers are believed to be at heightened risk for a number of stress-related physical illnesses, including hypertension and heart disease.[21] Early research also shows that pathological gamblers are at heightened risk for a variety of psychiatric disorders. For example, between 25 percent and 70 percent of individuals enrolled in Gamblers Anonymous or in one of the early inpatient treatment programs for problem gamblers sought help for another psychiatric problem.[22] These included depression and anxiety as well as panic disorders and mania.[23] Several recent community studies, including the U.S. national survey of gambling impacts and behavior, have found high rates of depression and suicidal ideation among problem gamblers in the community.[24] Researchers have argued that suicide attempt rates among pathological gamblers are higher than for any of the addictions and second only to suicide attempt rates among individuals with major affective disorder, schizophrenia, and a few hereditary disorders.[25]

There is significant overlap between problem and pathological gambling and addictive disorders such as alcohol and drug dependence. This is often referred to as co-morbidity. For example, the National Research Council notes that individuals admitted to chemical dependence treatment programs are three to six times more likely to be problem gamblers than individuals in the general population.[26] On the other side of the coin, large numbers of individuals who enter treatment for gambling problems report episodes of alcohol and drug abuse and dependence. A study in Minnesota found that one-third of the clients in the state's problem gambling treatment programs had received prior treatment for chemical dependency and 47 percent had received prior treatment for a mental health problem.[27]

Community research also has shown that problem gambling is associated with heavy use of alcohol and drugs.[28] For example, a telephone survey in New York found that problem gamblers were significantly more likely than nonproblem gamblers to use tobacco, alcohol, and drugs on a regular basis.[29] In studies of problem gamblers in communities in Canada and New Zealand, researchers found that individuals classified as pathological gamblers were significantly more likely than those without gambling problems to be smokers, heavy users of alcohol, and at least occasional users of illicit drugs.[30] The recent U.S. national survey found that problem and pathological gamblers were significantly more likely than others in the general population to have been alcohol- or drug-dependent at some time in their lives.[31]

FAMILY IMPACTS

Problem gamblers inflict substantial harm on their families, including spouses, children, parents, siblings, in-laws, and other relatives. Most of the research evidence, however, is limited to immediate family members. A survey of wives of Gamblers Anonymous members in the late 1970s found that these women experienced significant problems, including physical and psychological abuse and physical stress reactions.[32] Many spouses of pathological gamblers have high levels of depression as well as physical symptoms of stress, including chronic or severe headaches, stomach problems, dizziness, and breathing difficulties.[33] Rates of separation and divorce are significantly higher among problem and pathological gamblers in treatment and in the community than in the general population.[34]

Several recent surveys have found high rates of physical and verbal abuse among pathological gamblers in treatment as well as among problem gamblers in the community. For example, a study of family members of pathological gamblers in a Canadian treatment program found that 23 percent of spouses and 17 percent of children of these gamblers were physically abused.[35] Another treatment survey in Montana found that 27 percent of the pathological gamblers in self-help and professional treatment programs reported episodes of gambling-related domestic violence.[36] And a recent survey in North Dakota found that 92 percent of the small number of respondents who acknowledged having arguments about gambling that became physical were problem or pathological gamblers.[37]

Also within the family, there is evidence of a range of problems among the children of pathological gamblers. In addition to the physical abuse of children reported by members of Gamblers Anonymous and their spouses,[38] a study of California high school students found that adolescents who reported that one or both parents had a gambling problem reported higher levels of drug abuse and eating disorders than others in their schools. These youths also were more likely to report an unhappy childhood, to have legal action pending, and to be depressed and suicidal.[39] Similarly, in a study in New Jersey, students reporting a parental gambling problem were more likely than others in their schools to have a gambling problem of their own.[40]

WORKPLACE IMPACTS

There are numerous job-related impacts associated with problem and pathological gambling. These include irritability, moodiness and poor concentration at work, decreased efficiency, impaired judgment and faulty decisionmaking, gambling on company time, lateness and absences from work, and abuse of the telephone to place bets and deal with creditors. A recent survey of members of Gamblers Anonymous in Wisconsin found that these respondents had lost, on average, more than seven hours of work per month to their gambling.[41] Problem gamblers borrow money from other employees to gamble or to pay gambling-related debts, and this can affect the morale of their coworkers. Other job-related impacts include theft of company property and other illegal acts to obtain money through an employer.[42] The National Research Council noted that "roughly one-fourth to one-third of gamblers in . . . Gamblers Anonymous report the loss of their jobs due to gambling."[43]

FINANCIAL IMPACTS

Pathological gamblers in treatment tend to have considerable gambling-related debt. Early reports of average debt among pathological gamblers in treatment in the 1980s range widely, from $53,000 in New Jersey to $92,000 in Maryland.[44] More recently, the average lifetime gambling debt among clients in six Minnesota problem gambling treatment programs in 1996 was found to be $47,800, and the average gambling debt in the six months prior to treatment was $10,000. In spite of high levels of debt, only 29 percent of these clients reported annual household incomes over $30,000.[45]

Indebtedness affects not only pathological gamblers but also their families. For example, wives of Gamblers Anonymous members often report having to get loans or use credit cards to buy family essentials. These women also report frequent harassment and threats from bill collectors.[46]

Finally, problem gambling has been tied to bankruptcy. Recent surveys of Gamblers Anonymous members have found that between 18 and 28 percent of men and 8 percent of women had declared bankruptcy.[47] A review of bankruptcy filings in Minnesota found that gamblers filing for bankruptcy had an average of eight credit cards with balances of $5,000 to $10,000 each. These gamblers owed an average of $40,000 in unsecured debt; this did not include delinquent payments on mortgages, cars, or income taxes.[48]

LEGAL IMPACTS

Pathological gamblers in professional treatment and in self-help admit to a wide variety of illegal activities to obtain money to gamble or to pay gambling-related debts. These crimes are most often nonviolent and include passing bad checks, shoplifting, check forgery, thefts from employers, tax evasion and tax fraud, loan fraud, embezzlement, larceny, bookmaking, hustling, fencing stolen goods, and burglary.[49] A recent survey of Gamblers Anonymous members in Montana found that 69 percent of the respondents had "kited" checks to get money to gamble or pay gambling-related debts, and 73 percent admitted committing one or more illegal acts.[50] Many pathological gamblers entering treatment have significant legal problems, and there is evidence that many incarcerated individuals have problems related to their gambling.[51]

Although most crimes committed by problem gamblers are believed to be nonviolent, a recent analysis of links between gambling and crime, conducted for the Montana Gambling Study Commission, showed that burglary, larceny-theft, robbery, vandalism, driving under the influence, and weapons offenses were positively correlated with per capita tax revenues from video gaming machines throughout Montana. These relationships remained even after population differences were statistically controlled.[52]

THE COSTS OF PROBLEM GAMBLING

Until recently, most estimates of the social and economic impacts of problem gambling were based on information from individuals who had sought help for their gambling problems. This changed with the completion of a multifaceted research program in the United States, undertaken by the National Opinion Research Center at the University of Chicago on behalf of the National Gambling Impact Study Commission.[53] This commission, created by Congress in 1996, was charged with the task of assessing the scope and consequences of legal gambling in the United States. Estimates of the social and economic impacts of problem gambling were derived from a nationally representative telephone survey of adults and a separate intercept survey of patrons of gaming facilities.[54]

The national research team limited their analysis to those impacts that could be assigned an economic value and did not attempt to capture *all* of the impacts that might be important to an individual, family, or community. This is because many of the human burdens of problem gambling are not readily quantifiable. For example, the cost of legal fees in a divorce does not begin to capture all of the social and psychological pain of divorce for the partners and families directly involved. A further limitation is that no effort was made to assess the impacts of problem gambling experienced by individuals who did not meet the established cutoff levels for problem or pathological gambling. While individuals in this *at risk* group may experience only one or two difficulties before reducing their gambling or otherwise altering their involvement, the size of this group is so large that the overall impact of their problems could easily swamp the costs measured among problem or pathological gamblers who meet or exceed the cutoff points.

The initial step in the analysis was to develop a careful statistical protocol to enable the research team to analyze the data from the telephone interviews and the patron survey together. The next step involved comparing the rates of specific adverse consequences for each of several groups in the combined data set. These groups included nonproblem gamblers who did not score on any of the items in the problem gambling screen employed in the study, "problem" gamblers who scored 3 or 4 points on this screen, and "pathological" gamblers who scored 5 or more points on the screen.

The analysis used logistic regression to control for a variety of sociodemographic factors and to identify the "excessive" costs of a variety of difficulties experienced by problem gamblers beyond those experienced by nonproblem gamblers. These factors include gender, age, ethnic identity, education, region of the country, and problems with alcohol or drugs. The reason to control for these characteristics is that many of the impacts attributed to problem gambling are experienced by other people, whether or not they gamble. For example, we know that people who gamble heavily also tend to have alcohol and drug problems. Ignoring a person's alcohol and drug problems might lead researchers to mistakenly attribute some impacts and their costs to problem gambling alone.

Table 2.2 presents the proportion of nonproblem, problem, and pathological gamblers who acknowledged specific impacts that are believed to be associated with gambling-related difficulties. The table also presents *odds ratios,* which indicate how much more likely problem and pathological gamblers are to experience these consequences than similar individuals who gamble without difficulties.

TABLE 2.2. SUMMARY OF CONSEQUENCES OF PROBLEM GAMBLING

	RATE FOR NON-PROBLEM GAMBLERS (%)	RATE FOR PROBLEM GAMBLERS (%)	ODDS RATIO RELATIVE TO NON-PROBLEM GAMBLERS	RATE FOR PATHO-LOGICAL GAMBLERS (%)	ODDS RATIO RELATIVE TO NON-PROBLEM GAMBLERS
Job loss	4.0	10.8	2.07	13.8	2.62
Unemployment benefits	4.0	10.9	2.21	15.0	2.81
Welfare benefits	1.3	7.3	3.35	4.6	1.94
Bankruptcy	5.5	10.3	1.71	19.2	1.97
Divorce	29.8	39.5	1.38	53.5	2.29
Health poor or fair	13.9	16.4	n.s.	31.1	2.43
Use of mental health services	6.5	12.8	2.47	13.3	2.12
Arrest	11.1	36.3	3.15	32.3	2.00
Incarceration	4.0	10.5	2.34	21.4	4.38

Note: n.s. = not significant.
Source: Dean R. Gerstein et al., *Gambling Impact and Behavior Study: Report to the National Gambling Impact Study Commission* (Chicago: National Opinion Research Center, 1999), Chapter 3, Table 21, p. 58.

Table 2.2 shows that problem and pathological gamblers are significantly more likely than individuals who gamble recreationally to have suffered physical and psychological health problems, divorced, lost a job, been on welfare, declared bankruptcy, or been arrested and incarcerated. Consideration of the odds ratios shows that problem gamblers are 107 percent more likely and pathological gamblers are 162 percent more likely than nonproblem gamblers to have lost a job. Problem gamblers are 235 percent more likely than nonproblem gamblers to have received welfare benefits and 215 percent more likely to have been arrested. Pathological gamblers are 181 percent more likely than nonproblem gamblers to have received unemployment benefits and twice as likely to have been arrested. While pathological gamblers are slightly less likely than problem gamblers to have been arrested, they are more likely to have been incarcerated.

As Table 2.3 (page 18) shows, when dollar figures were applied to these ratios, the national research team concluded that the costs of problem and pathological gambling in the United States minus transfers to the gambler from creditors and other taxpayers are $560 and $1,050 per year, and $3,580 and $7,250 per lifetime, respectively. When these sums are multiplied by the estimated prevalence of problem and pathological gambling in the national survey, they translate into annual costs of about $4 billion per year, and about $28 billion on a lifetime basis. If transfers are included, the costs rise to about $5 billion per year and $40 billion on a lifetime basis.

Compared with economic cost estimates for other disorders, the estimates for problem and pathological gambling appear low. For example, the annual cost estimate for problem and pathological gambling in 1998 of $5 billion compares with 1995 estimates for drug abuse of $110 billion and for alcohol abuse of $166 billion.[55] One reason for this difference is the cost of treatment for these disorders, which is far more easily available and sought far more often by sufferers of drug and alcohol abuse than by problem gamblers. Since health care accounts for about one-half of the economic impact of these disorders, as the U.S. national research team notes, "the measured economic impacts therefore include the cost of society's determination to respond directly to such problems."[56]

Another reason for the relatively low cost of problem and pathological gambling compared with other disorders lies in the difficulty of "annualizing" some costs. Some impacts, such as divorce and bankruptcy, are relatively rare events, and better information about the average duration of problem and pathological gambling in the general population is needed to allocate these lifetime costs over a period of time. It is worth stressing that the impacts of problem and pathological gambling considered by the

TABLE 2.3. COSTS OF SOCIAL AND ECONOMIC IMPACTS OF PROBLEM GAMBLING

	WHO PAYS (PRIMARY)	PROBLEM GAMBLER COSTS		PATHOLOGICAL GAMBLER COSTS	
		LIFETIME	PAST YEAR	LIFETIME	PAST YEAR
Job loss	Employer	n.e.	$200	n.e.	$320
Unemployment benefits	Government	n.e.	$65	n.e.	$85
Welfare benefits	Government	n.e.	$90	n.e.	$60
Bankruptcy	Creditors	$1,550	n.e.	$3,300	n.e.
Divorce	Gambler/ spouse	$1,950	n.e.	$4,300	n.e.
Poor health	Health insurance	n.e.	$0	n.e.	$700
Poor mental health	Health insurance	n.e.	$360[a]	n.e.	($330)[b]
Arrests	Government	$960	n.e.	$1,250	n.e.
Corrections (incarceration)	Government	$670	n.e.	$1,700	n.e.
Gambling treatment	Government	$0	$0	n.e.	$30
Total costs/impacts		$5,130	$715	$10,550	$1,195
Costs minus transfers		$3,580	$560	$7,250	$1,050
Transfers to gamblers		$1,550	$155	$3,300	$145

[a] net increase in cost.
[b] part of total health.
Note: n.e. = not able to be estimated in this survey.

Source: Dean R. Gerstein et al., *Gambling Impact and Behavior Study: Report to the National Gambling Impact Study Commission* (Chicago: National Opinion Research Center, 1999), Chapter 3, Table 19, p. 52.

national research team represent only those most readily quantifiable and probably understate the true social costs of these disorders. Although many social costs are difficult to quantify, jury awards in tobacco and other liability cases make it clear that these costs are valued highly in our society.

WHAT CAUSES PROBLEM GAMBLING?

Theories about problem gambling tend to fall into three general categories: the *individual susceptibility* model, which assumes that there are factors unique to the individual that explain the development of a pathological style of gambling; the *motivational* model, which remains focused on the individual but emphasizes the relationship of an individual's type and style of gambling to the development of gambling problems; and the *sociological* model, which is similar to social learning models but with an emphasis on gambling settings rather than on problem gamblers in treatment.

The majority of theories about problem gambling emphasize *individual susceptibility* in the development of pathological gambling. These theories fall into several categories. Relying on genetic and neurophysiological evidence, biological theorists view gambling problems as the result of a physiological condition (that is, an imbalance in the chemicals that affect the brain) that lead the individual to experience an aroused, physiological response to gambling.[57] Some researchers who subscribe to biological theories view pathological gambling as an inherited susceptibility, rather than as a disease. Like the biological theories, the medical, or "disease," model of problem gambling sees qualitative differences between nonproblem and problem gamblers and views problem gambling as a progressive and irreversible condition.[58] Psychodynamic, or psychoanalytic, models of problem gambling also locate pathological gambling squarely within the individual psyche, arguing that pathological gambling is a self-medicating response to psychic pain.[59]

Personality, or trait, theories link pathological gambling to individual psychological profiles.[60] For example, pathological gambling is frequently associated with depression and with antisocial personality disorder among individuals in treatment. There is debate, however, regarding which disorder is the cause and which is the effect—debates complicated by the fact that there is evidence to support both hypotheses.[61]

Theorists who focus on individual susceptibility tend to stress the importance of gambling in helping some people cope with negative emotions that stem from psychological or physiological discomfort. The notion that childhood trauma can set the stage for later development of gambling-related difficulties, at least for female pathological gamblers, is one facet of this approach.[62] Other researchers emphasize the role of a parent, either in not providing an adequate rearing environment or by serving as a gambling role model.[63] Still others view pathological gambling as one manifestation of a common underlying vulnerability to a variety of addictive disorders. Pathological gamblers are believed to become dependent on an aroused euphoric state similar to a drug-induced high.[64] Recent work on the biochemical and genetic basis for pathological gambling supports the notion of a combination of impulsive-addictive-compulsive behaviors that are associated with specific genetic variations.[65]

Theories that stress individual susceptibility in the development of pathological gambling have been criticized as reductionist and tautological. Other criticisms center on the implications that such models have for the willingness of individuals to seek help and on how such models shift responsibility for achieving recovery from the "sick" individual to the "expert" physician.[66] Many of these individual susceptibility theories were developed by researchers working in clinical settings with the most severely affected pathological gamblers and may not be appropriate for individuals with less severe gambling problems.

Motivational models encompass social learning theories and cognitive-behavioral approaches as well as some social psychological models. Social learning theorists view gambling as a learned behavior with involvement determined largely by social context or environment.[67] In contrast to biological and medical models, social learning models suggest that gambling behavior falls along a continuum, from problem-free to problem-dominated gambling, without predictable stages and without assumptions of irreversibility. From the social learning perspective, gambling behavior is acquired through classical behavioral conditioning with variable reinforcement schedules, which are especially powerful when combined with financial rewards and heightened levels of arousal.

Cognitive-behavioral theories are similar to learning theories but with a focus on the role of cognitive processes in the acquisition and maintenance of gambling behavior.[68] In contrast to social learning models, which are behaviorally focused, cognitive theories emphasize the importance of biases, including the illusion of control, biased evaluations, and the reinforcing properties of the near miss, in the development of problem gambling.[69]

Motivational models center on the interaction between susceptible individuals and different gambling activities. They emphasize the specific features of different gambling activities that may play a role in the loss of control over gambling.[70] Recent research on the cognitive distortions associated with different types of gambling is one example of the effort to understand pathological gambling as a mediation between individuals and specific gambling activities.[71] Another important focus of this approach is the reasons that problem gamblers have for their gambling. For example, while some problem gamblers indicate that their major reason for continuing to gamble is to "stay in action,"[72] others look upon their gambling as a means of escape from overwhelming personal problems.[73]

In some ways, *sociological* theories are similar to the motivational models. However, the focus in sociological models is on gambling settings rather than on problem gamblers as individuals. Sociological theories have emerged largely from the participant-observation tradition in sociology and, like motivational models, view gambling behavior as a continuum—problem gambling may lie at one end of the continuum, but it is not qualitatively different from nonproblem gambling. The importance of particular social contexts in providing opportunities for taking on exciting social roles and for obtaining social rewards are the focus of many sociological analyses of gambling.[74]

The strengths of the motivational and sociological models of problem gambling lie in the focus on environmental and cultural factors that influence gambling behavior as well as the effects of external social factors on individual behavior. Another strength of these models is their recognition that gambling problems lie on a continuum. Motivational models have contributed to the development of specific treatment interventions; a critical weakness of the sociological theories is that, to date, they have contributed little to improving the prevention and treatment of problem gambling.

It is likely that problem gambling represents a mix of individual susceptibilities and motivations as well as social settings. It is also likely that there are different "types" of problem gamblers with different individual susceptibilities at the beginning of their gambling careers and different motivations to continue their gambling once they have started.[75] Many gambling researchers now agree that gambling problems are best conceptualized as a combination of biological, psychological, and social factors,[76] and most disagreements stem from differences in the emphasis placed on individual versus social or environmental factors that may contribute to problem gambling. In

spite of broad agreement about the nature of problem and pathological gambling, the National Research Council recently concluded that
a great deal of research was still needed to understand the causes and
progression of this disorder.[77]

WHAT ARE WE LEAVING OUT?

There are many issues related to problem gambling that are beyond
the scope of this report. One of these is the question of gambling problems among underage youths. There are several reasons for this omis-
sion. One is that, although age limits vary considerably for different
games and in different states, nearly all of the gambling done by youths
is illegal. There are also uncertainties about the best approach to measuring gambling problems among young people. While studies have
established that gambling problems among youths (measured with tools
developed for adults) are often quite high, it appears that only a small
proportion of those who gamble, and even of those who experience
substantial gambling-related problems in adolescence, progress to more
serious difficulties. Until we know more about how young people experience gambling problems and how their experiences with gambling
are similar or different from those of older cohorts in the population, it
seems best to leave consideration of youth gambling for another day.

Another issue that is addressed only peripherally here is the often
tacit notion that problem gambling is the same as regular, heavy, or
inveterate gambling. While many problem gamblers are often heavy
gamblers, the converse is not always true. There are individuals who
gamble regularly, and even heavily, but do not lose control over their
gambling, exhibit a progression in their gambling participation or in
their efforts to obtain money to gamble, or experience adverse consequences related to their gambling. Many of these individuals prefer
gambling activities that feature strong elements of subjective proba-
bility, such as horse race and sports wagering, and some of them
make a very good living as professional gamblers.[78] Others, as John
Rosecrance has pointed out, love gambling and have made conscious
decisions that enable them to maintain that way of life.[79] While inveterate gamblers present intriguing challenges for researchers,[80] our
focus in the current context is on individuals who experience problems related to their gambling rather than on heavy gambling per se.

3

LEGAL GAMBLING AND THE
EMERGENCE OF PROBLEM
GAMBLING

Chapter 2 noted that the contemporary view of problem and pathological gambling in America as a medical issue emerged from the intersection of two unique social and historical developments at the end of the twentieth century. These developments were, first, the rapid legalization of lotteries and casinos throughout the United States and, second, changes in the American health care system that led to an expansion of the conditions for which therapists could obtain reimbursement for mental health treatment.[1] This chapter examines these social and historical developments in more detail.

To begin, it is important to recognize that "gambling" is a broad concept that includes diverse activities, undertaken in a wide variety of settings, appealing to different sorts of people and perceived in various ways by participants and observers. Both gambling participation and attitudes toward gambling are linked to the communities in which these behaviors occur and to the norms and values of members of those communities. Individuals and communities have different definitions of gambling—for example, a recent Gallup poll found that 52 percent of respondents defined stock market investment as a form of gambling while 22 percent did not consider buying state-sponsored lottery tickets to be gambling.[2] Furthermore, different groups in American society—men and women, middle class and blue collar, white, black, and Asian—have preferences for different types of gambling.[3]

THE RECENT EVOLUTION OF LEGAL GAMBLING

Longstanding ambivalence characterizes the history of gambling in the United States, as successive waves of leniency alternated with severe repression.[4] In the early nineteenth century, the risky and transient society of river towns and steamboats along the lower Mississippi River fostered the emergence of professional gamblers and new games characterized by speed and portability, including card games such as faro, *vingt-et-un*, and poker as well as roulette and dice games. In the mid-nineteenth century, as newly settled areas sought to emulate more established and respectable communities in the East, professional gamblers became the focus of violent popular justice throughout the Southwest. In the same period, casino gambling flourished on the mining frontier in California and the newly popular gambling games were introduced by syndicates to cities in the East.[5] It was not until the end of the nineteenth century, with the ascendancy of Victorian respectability and the spectacular collapse of the Louisiana Lottery, that casino games and lotteries were outlawed throughout the United States. In the wake of federal legislation intended to eliminate fraudulent games, legal gambling opportunities were heavily restricted throughout the United States and remained so for most of the twentieth century.[6]

In 1976, at the beginning of the most recent wave of gambling legalization, only thirteen states had lotteries, two states (Nevada and New York) had approved off-track wagering, and there were no casinos outside of Nevada.[7] The gambling industry has grown tenfold since the Commission on the Review of the National Policy Toward Gambling sponsored the first comprehensive national survey on American gambling behavior, in 1975. Today, a person can make a legal wager of some sort in every state except Utah, Tennessee, and Hawaii; thirty-seven states have lotteries, twenty-eight states have casinos, and twenty-two have off-track betting.[8]

Just as telling as the expansion of gambling into new jurisdictions is the growth in the revenues of the gambling industries. Between 1975 and 1999, revenues from legal wagering in the United States grew by nearly 1,800 percent, from $3 billion to $58 billion.[9]

Americans now spend more on legal gambling than they spend on movie tickets, recorded music, theme parks, spectator sports, and video games combined on an annual basis.[10]

Much of the initiative for the legalization of lotteries in the 1970s and 1980s grew out of the reluctance of state legislatures to raise taxes. In legalizing lotteries, measures often were taken to earmark funds from this newly legal form of gambling for specific purposes: education, property tax relief, or services for seniors. The forces driving the legalization of casino gambling are rather different from those driving the legalization of lotteries. In addition to rising state and local revenue needs, casino legalization was powered by the passage of the Indian Gaming Regulatory Act of 1988 and by economic recession in the midwestern states.

Another important factor in the process of casino legalization was the shift in ownership and control of casinos and casino companies, from shady, "mob" businesses to publicly owned, publicly traded corporations.[11] In the 1950s and 1960s, the spotlight on gambling focused on the links between casinos and organized crime.[12] In response, the casino industry in Nevada was slowly restructured along corporate lines, using the principles of industrial integration, mass production, economies of scale, standardization of prices, wagers, and odds, and sophisticated publicity campaigns. During the late 1960s and 1970s, corporate investors such as Howard Hughes, Kirk Kerkorian, and Merv Griffin, as well as Hilton Hotels, Metro-Goldwyn-Mayer, and Holiday Inns, placed the casino industry on a more legitimate footing.[13]

As the National Gambling Impact Study Commission noted, "the gambling 'industry' is far from monolithic," and each segment—casinos, lotteries, pari-mutuel wagering, sports wagering, charitable gambling, electronic gambling devices, and Internet gambling—"has its own distinct set of issues, communities of interests, and balance sheet of assets and liabilities."[14] The phenomenal growth in this sector of the economy largely has been fueled by the development of the lottery and casino industries at the expense of older, more mature industries such as pari-mutuel wagering and charitable gambling. Figures 3.1A and 3.1B (pages 26–27) demonstrates vividly how the availability of lottery and casino gambling has increased in America over the past twenty-five years.

The introduction of lottery and casino gambling in new jurisdictions tends to follow a predictable trajectory. Extremely high initial

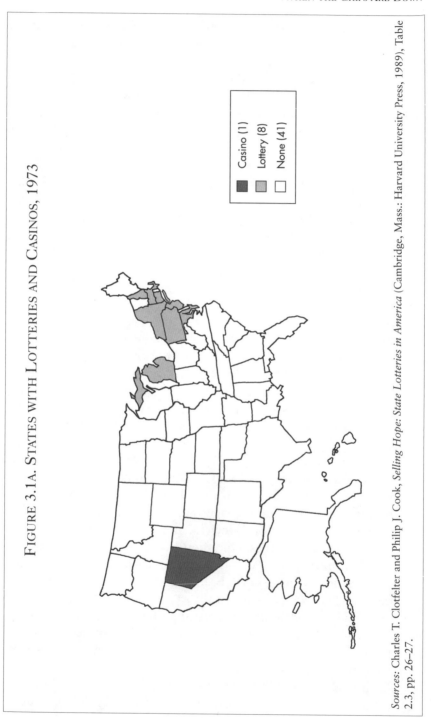

FIGURE 3.1A. STATES WITH LOTTERIES AND CASINOS, 1973

Casino (1)
Lottery (8)
None (41)

Sources: Charles T. Clotfelter and Philip J. Cook, *Selling Hope: State Lotteries in America* (Cambridge, Mass.: Harvard University Press, 1989), Table 2.3, pp. 26–27.

FIGURE 3.1B. STATES WITH LOTTERIES AND CASINOS, 1999

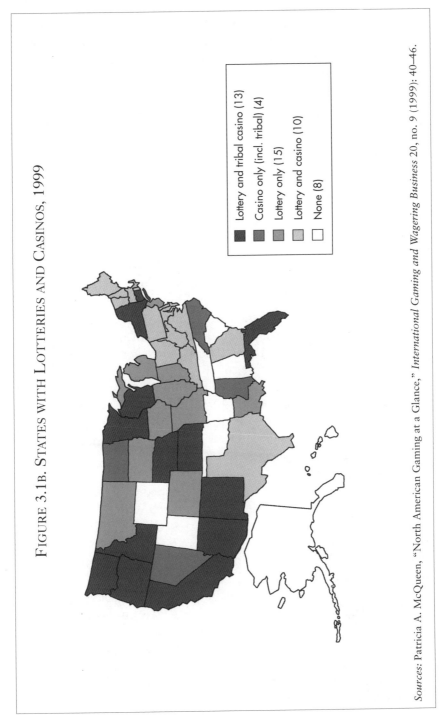

Lottery and tribal casino (13)

Casino only (incl. tribal) (4)

Lottery only (15)

Lottery and casino (10)

None (8)

Sources: Patricia A. McQueen, "North American Gaming at a Glance," *International Gaming and Wagering Business* 20, no. 9 (1999): 40–46.

participation is followed by stabilization and then by the introduction of new games to revive interest and increase expenditures. Another common pattern is the seeking of regulatory concessions by established gaming operators to maintain a "level playing field" in the face of new competition.[15] Attempts to level the playing field have generally been adopted on behalf of the least successful sectors of the gambling industry (that is, charitable gambling and pari-mutuel wagering). Examples include tax relief provisions for racetracks as well as the expansion of pari-mutuel wagering to include off-track and telephone betting and the introduction of slot machines and card rooms at racetracks. In response to the rapid expansion of casino-style gambling on tribal reservations, charitable gambling operators in many states have been permitted to conduct linked, progressive bingo games, and licensed card rooms have been allowed to establish "house banked" games. Limits on bet size and total losses, as well as requirements for cruising, were lifted for riverboats in Iowa in response to competition from dockside gambling operations in Illinois. More recently, limits on bets at casinos in Deadwood, South Dakota, were lifted in response to regional competition from tribal casinos. The practical impact of all of these actions, however, is to expand the availability of gambling further.

Although public attitudes toward gambling have become more accepting, grassroots opposition to legal gambling began to emerge in the mid-1990s as coalitions of citizens' groups formed to prevent or repeal these increasingly ubiquitous activities. Grassroots organizations have had varying success in opposing specific gambling proposals in different states. While opposition to gambling initiatives has been characterized as "sporadic, poorly funded, and directed toward a particular piece of legislation," this changed with the formation of the National Coalition Against Legalized Gambling in 1994. This organization, founded by Reverend Tom Grey, a Methodist minister from Illinois, "has successfully lobbied in several states against specific initiatives to introduce or to expand gambling."[16]

In the United States as well as internationally, groups opposed to gambling legalization have been most effective in working to limit the availability of electronic gambling machines. In South Dakota, several recent elections have included referenda to repeal video lottery terminals, although none have passed. In a recent statewide referendum, nearly half of the parishes in Louisiana voted to ban video poker machines. In South Carolina, a grassroots campaign was successful in shutting down thousands of video poker machines operating throughout the state. Even in Las Vegas the mayor established a committee to consider removing slot and video poker machines from neighborhood businesses.[17]

It is possible that we are seeing the beginnings of another broad wave of gambling restriction in the United States. However, as our history with Prohibition shows, there are difficulties in making any widespread behavior illegal. Laws against gambling are difficult to enforce because so many people engage in these activities. Furthermore, governments now permit many types of gambling and it is difficult for citizens to make distinctions between similar activities, only one of which is sanctioned by the state. For example, many governments permit lotteries while, at the same time, prohibiting "numbers" or "policy" games (essentially, illegal lotteries). In legalizing gaming machines, many governments have made the argument that illegal, "gray" machines will be put out of business. However, citizens find it hard to distinguish between machines owned by the government and those owned by other, sometimes illegal, operators.

The incentive for gambling legalization in the United States in the 1980s and 1990s was largely economic. Governments are nearly always in need of revenues and there are certain historical moments when the incentive for revenues is particularly great: one such moment in the United States came in the 1980s, when federal funding to states was cut sharply. Gambling legalization began with promises of tax revenues and, later, jobs and economic development. In an era of federal budget cuts and economic restructuring, state and local governments found these promises very appealing, as the rapid spread of lotteries, and later casino gambling, across the United States attests. In support of legalization, gambling operators and politicians needed to overcome the stereotypes of gambling as a "deviant" behavior and of operators as "organized crime." Operators and legislators promoted the view that "gambling is a rational behavior . . . [that has] lost the moral overtones that past generations held over it" and that the gambling industry was, for the most part, "a benign business institution."[18]

Broad changes in American society followed the establishment of legal gambling as part of everyday life. The operation and oversight of gambling activities became part of the routine processes of government. Gambling commissions were established and regulators hired and trained; constituencies of customers, workers, and suppliers emerged. Governments became dependent on revenues from legal

gambling to fund essential services. To varying degrees, so did church-
es, voluntary and charitable organizations, the mass media and, more
recently, researchers and gambling treatment providers—sectors that
have traditionally served as critics and the conscience of society. Many
nongambling occupations and businesses also became increasingly
dependent on legal gambling. In particular, convenience stores, retail
operators, restaurants, hotels, and social clubs have grown dependent on revenues from legal gambling to continue to operate prof-
itably. Most recently, gambling industry executives and political action
committees became key sources of funding for political parties, elections, and ballot initiatives.

The New Gamblers in America

Gambling among the upper classes, whether on horses, cards, casino
games, real estate, or stocks, has long been condoned in most Western
societies. Despite the efforts of reformers, similar activities have been
broadly tolerated among the working and lower classes. In contrast,
until the latter part of the twentieth century, gambling among the
middle classes was widely discouraged. Over a decade ago, John
Rosecrance argued that the rapid legalization of gambling would lead
to growth in the gambling participation of the middle classes. Given
the size and influence of the middle class in American society,
Rosecrance believed that their acceptance of legal gambling would
be an important factor in the continued expansion of lotteries, casinos, and pari-mutuel wagering in the United States.[19] The results of
the two national studies of gambling that have been carried out in the
United States are evidence that Rosecrance was correct.

The first survey was done by the Institute for Social Research at
the University of Michigan in 1975 on behalf of the Commission on
the Review of the National Policy Toward Gambling.[20] The second
was carried out by the National Opinion Research Center at the
University of Chicago in 1998 on behalf of the National Gambling
Impact Study Commission.[21] Although the 1975 and 1998 surveys
used somewhat different methodologies, they were sufficiently similar to enable some comparisons to be made.

While there was substantial social acceptance of gambling long
before most Americans had access to legal gambling opportunities,
gambling participation has increased as access has grown. A Gallup

poll in 1950 estimated that 57 percent of the American population had gambled at least once.[22] In 1975, the first national survey of gambling in the United States showed that 68 percent of adults had gambled at some point in their lives; the second national survey in 1998 found that 86 percent of adults had done so.[23]

In contrast to lifetime participation, past-year gambling participation rates have not changed much since 1975. The proportion of respondents in the two national surveys indicating that they had gambled in the past year barely changed between 1975 and 1998, rising from 61 percent to 63 percent. Americans in 1998 were far more likely to participate in casino and lottery gambling, which are widely advertised and highly visible, and much less likely to participate in older types of gambling with less visibility, such as bingo and horse race wagering. In 1998, the percentage of people who reported playing the lottery in the past year was two times the percentage in 1975, while the increase in the percentage of respondents who reported gambling in a casino in the past year was even greater. In contrast, past-year bingo participation and past-year participation in horse race wagering both decreased by two-thirds between 1975 and 1998.[24]

GENDER AND GAMBLING

In 1975, the types and amount of gambling done by men and women were quite different. The 1975 national survey found that 68 percent of males and 55 percent of females participated in all types of gambling. As the availability of legal gambling has grown in America, however, women's gambling has started to look more like the gambling done by men. Table 3.1 (page 32) shows that while men still gamble more than women, the difference between the genders has narrowed to only a few percentage points. As Table 3.2 (page 33) illustrates, past-year casino and lottery players are just as likely to be women as men.

In contrast to legal forms, women are far less likely than men to participate in *illegal* types of gambling.[25] In 1975, 17 percent of males and only 5 percent of females participated in illegal types of gambling.[26] In 1998, men were still more likely than women to engage in illegal forms of gambling—men in the 1998 survey were significantly more likely than women to gamble in card rooms and at unlicensed gambling establishments and to participate in private wagers among

TABLE 3.1. LIFETIME, PAST-YEAR, AND WEEKLY
GAMBLING BY GENDER, AGE, AND ETHNICITY (%)

	EVER	PAST YEAR	WEEKLY
Total	85.6	63.3	16.3
Male	88.1	67.6	20.9
Female	83.2	59.3	12.0
18–29	83.7	65.2	11.8
30–39	87.5	66.2	15.7
40–49	90.2	66.6	15.5
50–64	86.1	65.7	21.4
65+	79.8	50.0	18.9
White	87.5	65.1	15.4
Black	77.7	56.4	22.3
Other	83.1	60.4	15.4

Source: Gambling Impact and Behavior Survey, Public Use File (weighted RDD-patron sample), data available through the Inter-University Consortium for Political and Social Research at the University of Michigan, available at http://www.icpsr.umich.edu/SAMHDA/fasttrack.html.

themselves. The only type of gambling that women are more likely than men to participate in is bingo.

As with illegal gambling, the scope of women's gambling—that is, the number of gambling activities in which they participate—is more limited than that of men. A 1989 telephone survey of Iowa adults found that while women were not significantly different from men in the frequency of their gambling, the amounts they wagered, or the time they spent gambling, they engaged in significantly fewer gambling activities than men.[27] An analysis of gambling participation among citizens of four states surveyed between 1992 and 1994 also found that women were less likely to participate in multiple gambling domains than men.[28]

AGE AND GAMBLING

Together, age and gender are the strongest demographic predictors of participation in specific types of gambling. Like the gambling of women compared with men, older Americans are less likely than

TABLE 3.2. PAST-YEAR GAMBLING PARTICIPATION BY GENDER, AGE, AND ETHNICITY (%)

	MALE	FEMALE	18–29	30–39	40–49	50–64	65+	WHITE	BLACK	OTHER
Casino	27.0	24.4	25.6	26.2	26.3	31.5	17.8	26.1	24.0	24.6
Track	9.5	6.8	8.2	7.1	8.8	9.5	7.2	8.2	7.9	7.6
Lottery	55.3	47.9	49.1	55.7	56.2	55.8	38.5	52.4	47.7	49.7
Bingo	3.0	6.8	6.3	4.8	3.8	5.3	4.8	4.8	3.3	7.6
Charitable	4.6	4.3	3.9	4.4	4.1	6.5	3.3	5.3	1.1	2.8
Card rooms	3.2	0.5	3.9	1.6	1.2	1.6	0.4	2.2	0.8	1.0
Private	14.4	5.7	18.2	10.6	7.0	6.9	4.1	10.9	4.4	9.8
Store	10.1	5.7	9.4	9.3	6.9	9.7	2.8	8.9	5.7	4.0
Unlicensed	9.8	5.7	10.5	8.0	9.1	7.1	2.2	9.0	3.3	4.8
Indian	7.1	5.8	6.0	7.8	4.6	8.9	4.3	7.5	1.9	4.3

Source: Gambling Impact and Behavior Survey, Public Use File (weighted RDD-patron sample), data available through the Inter-University Consortium for Political and Social Research at the University of Michigan, available at http://www.icpsr.umich.edu/SAMHDA/fasttrack.html.

younger Americans to gamble. Furthermore, when older Americans do gamble, they tend to be involved in fewer activities than younger Americans.[29]

The 1998 national survey found that while lifetime gambling participation had increased for all age groups since 1975, the increase was far more dramatic for older adults than for younger adults. In contrast to lifetime gambling, past-year gambling participation actually decreased among young adults, but it increased among adults ages 45 to 64 and doubled among persons ages 65 and over. In spite of this increase, seniors are still underrepresented in the total population of past-year gamblers.

The picture becomes more complicated when we examine the types of gambling in which people of different ages are likely to participate. As Table 3.2 shows, with only a few exceptions, past-year participation in specific types of gambling is highest among adults ages 30 to 64 and lowest among adults ages 65 and over. Adults ages 50 to 64 are substantially more likely than individuals in other age groups to have engaged in charitable gambling and to have gambled at an Indian casino or bingo hall. In contrast, adults ages 18 to 29 are substantially more likely than older adults to have gambled privately. Adults ages 65 and over are the group least likely to have gambled privately, at an unlicensed establishment, or at a store, bar, restaurant, truck stop, or similar location.

While older adults are less likely than younger adults to have ever gambled or to have gambled in the past year, these individuals are just as likely—if not more likely—to gamble weekly. As Table 3.1 shows, 12 percent of adults ages 18 to 29 and 16 percent of adults ages 30 to 49 acknowledged gambling weekly; in contrast, 21 percent of adults ages 50 to 64 and 19 percent of adults ages 65 and over gamble weekly on one or more activities.

ETHNICITY AND GAMBLING

While gender and age are strong predictors of gambling, ethnicity also plays a role. Table 3.1 shows that lifetime and past-year gambling participation rates are significantly higher for whites than for other racial and ethnic groups in the United States. Meanwhile, weekly gambling participation is highest among African Americans. Still, there are substantial differences in the proportions of men and women in these ethnic groups who gamble: while 29 percent of black men and 21 percent of white men gamble weekly, only 17 percent of black women and 11 percent of white women gamble this frequently.

When it comes to participation in particular types of gambling, Table 3.2 shows that adults from all ethnic groups are equally likely to have gambled in the past year on the lottery, at a casino, or on a horse or dog race. However, white adults are substantially more likely than adults from other ethnic groups to have gambled in the past year on a charitable event, at a store, bar, or restaurant that offered only one gambling activity (usually video poker or some other type of gaming machine), at an unlicensed establishment, or at a tribal gaming operation. Nonwhite adults are more likely than whites to have gambled in the past year on bingo. Black adults are the least likely to have gambled in the past year on private types of wagering, such as card games in someone's home or on games of personal skill.

ATTITUDES TOWARD GAMBLING

Although gambling participation has increased since 1975, attitudes toward gambling have not changed dramatically in the United States. Most Americans hold complex and ambivalent rather than simple pro or anti attitudes about the effects of gambling on society. A Gallup survey in 1999 found that 29 percent of adults felt that gambling is immoral, compared with 27 percent in 1996 and 32 percent in 1992.[30] The same survey found that only 22 percent of adults favored further expansion of legal gambling, while 47 percent favored the status quo and 29 percent wanted legal gambling opportunities reduced or banned outright. The reason for this general disinclination for the expansion of gambling was evidently that, while 67 percent of adults felt that casinos generally help a community's economy, 56 percent believed that casinos damage everyday family and community life.

As with gambling participation, age is a strong demographic predictor of attitudes toward gambling. On a five-point scale from very good to very bad, only 25 percent of eighteen- to twenty-nine-year-olds consider the overall effects of legalized gambling on society to be bad or very bad, a percentage that rises steadily by age group, reaching 56 percent among those sixty-five and older. There are no significant differences in this attitude by income or ethnicity, and only slight differences by sex and education, with males and those with less than a high school education tending to be slightly more positive about gambling's social effects.[31]

While attitudes toward gambling remain complex, the reasons why people gamble have changed in the United States since 1975. The percentage of people who said they gambled in order to win money increased by one-half between 1975 and 1998, from 44 to 66 percent. In contrast, the percentage who said they gambled for excitement or challenge decreased by almost one-third, from 70 to 49 percent. The 1998 numbers tell a similar story to those of a 1993 Roper survey, which found that 75 percent of casino patrons said the primary reason they visit casinos is to win "a really large amount of money," while only 57 percent said that entertainment and recreation were important reasons they visit casinos.[32] Americans in the 1990s and the new millennium appear to gamble less for the sheer joy of it and more as though it were a nonsalaried second job, like day-trading or selling real estate. While people are now more likely to gamble in order to win money, the fact remains that most people who gamble, and especially those who gamble regularly, are most likely to lose money over the long run.

Reasons for gambling, like participation, vary by gender, age, and ethnicity. For example, men are more likely than women, and young adults (those ages eighteen to twenty-nine) are more likely than older adults, to say that they gamble for excitement. Young adults are also much more likely than adults ages sixty-five and older to say that winning money is an important reason to gamble. Among different racial and ethnic groups, Hispanics are more likely than blacks to say that they gamble in order to socialize, while blacks are more likely than whites or Hispanics to say that they gamble in order to win money. There are also ethnic differences in the reasons that nongamblers give for *not* gambling: only 29 percent of Hispanic nongamblers, versus 49 percent of black nongamblers and 58 percent of white nongamblers, refrained from gambling for moral reasons. Meanwhile, 72 percent of black nongamblers and 67 percent of white nongamblers—but only 54 percent of Hispanic nongamblers—refrained for financial reasons. These data suggest that Hispanics tend to approach gambling more as a social activity, and blacks more as a financial proposition.

WHERE IS LEGAL GAMBLING HEADED?

It is difficult to forecast the evolution of legal gambling in America through the first decades of the twenty-first century. There are several trends that will influence this evolution, occasionally in opposite directions, including heightened participation of the middle class in legal forms of gambling, the spread of gambling to nongambling settings, and the looming impacts of gambling on the Internet.[33] Other trends that may influence the evolution of legal gambling in the United States will be the continued availability of different types of gambling and concomitant changes in participation as people balance their gambling with other pursuits that they consider important.

Beyond the expansion in the availability of casinos and lotteries, the most notable change in Americans' access to gambling in the last two decades has been the shift in the availability of gambling from gambling-specific venues to a much wider range of social settings. Many forms of gambling, but especially electronic gaming devices (EGDs), are now available in bars, restaurants, hotels, social clubs, grocery and convenience stores, and even Laundromats—places where gambling was never previously available. Many of these operations have, in effect, become mini-casinos and sometimes are promoted as such.

While the consequences of this diffusion of gambling throughout society have yet to be adequately examined, convenience gambling was roundly condemned in the recent final report of the National Gambling Impact Study Commission.[34] Certainly, the widespread appeal of EGDs to women and middle-class gamblers suggests that gambling participation rates will continue to increase, particularly in states where this type of gambling is introduced.

In contrast, the results of recent replication studies in several regions of the United States suggest that gambling participation may be declining.[35] All of these data are drawn from telephone surveys with randomly selected respondents in the adult population, and all used similarly structured questionnaires that included questions about lifetime, past-year, and weekly gambling on a range of activities. Figure 3.2 (page 38) presents information about the magnitude of changes in the proportion of respondents in each of five jurisdictions who have never gambled, who have gambled in the past year but not weekly, and who gamble weekly. These changes are

FIGURE 3.2. CHANGES IN GAMBLING PARTICIPATION ACROSS SELECTED U.S. JURISDICTIONS

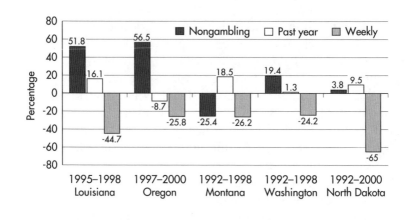

Source: Rachel A. Volberg, *Changes in Gambling and Problem Gambling in Oregon, 1997 to 2000,* report to the Oregon Gambling Addiction Treatment Foundation (Salem: Oregon Gambling Addiction Treatment Foundation, 2001), Figure 1, p. 23.

presented in terms of magnitude rather than as changes in percentages in order to compare "apples with apples."[36] The results are arrayed according to the interval between the baseline and the replication survey in each state.

The figure shows that the proportion of respondents who were nongamblers increased in four of the five states under consideration. Similarly, the proportion of respondents who had gambled in the past year but did not gamble on a weekly basis increased in four of the five states. The clearest pattern in these data is that the proportion of respondents who gamble weekly or more often on one or more types of gambling decreased substantially in all five jurisdictions. While the decline was greatest in North Dakota between 1992 and 2000 and smallest in Washington State between 1992 and 1998, the declines in all of these jurisdictions were statistically significant. These data suggest that gambling participation rates may decline over time as people experiment with different activities and then stabilize their involvement to balance it with other important parts of their lives, including work and family commitments.

A final potential trend that will affect gambling participation is the looming impact of the Internet. Commercial gambling on the Internet, including blackjack, slot machines, bingo, keno, craps, horse and dog races, sports events, and lottery games, is now available on more than one thousand websites owned by 250 to 300 parent businesses or government agencies. Global consumer spending on Internet gambling is expected to reach $6.3 billion by 2003. There are a number of factors powering the development of Internet gambling, including consumer demand, the arrival of name brands, internal gambling industry pressures, the consumer price advantages created by the location of e-gambling businesses in tax havens, and the enabling technology of the Internet itself.[37] The Internet has the potential to be the strongest growth market for legal gambling over the next ten to twenty years. Internet gambling sites are multiplying rapidly, and more and more countries are legalizing these activities and bringing them under regulatory control. Examples include not only remote Caribbean and Mediterranean islands, but also major industrialized nations, such as Great Britain and Australia.

In the United States, in spite of the proposed Internet Gambling Prohibition Act, a recent conviction of an off-shore sports book operator, and the National Gambling Impact Study Commission's recommendation that Congress criminalize Internet gambling, market forces are overwhelming legislative and judicial efforts to halt the migration of gamblers to cyberspace. Unsure of its legality and concerned for their licenses, established gambling suppliers in the United States have hesitated to embrace Internet gambling. Consumers have been less discriminating—a recent study in Oregon found that participation in all types of gambling, including casino and lottery games, had declined or remained stable between 1997 and 2000 with one exception: although starting from an extremely low base rate in 1997, lifetime Internet gambling participation increased by 260 percent and past-year Internet gambling grew by 600 percent.[38]

It may be possible to discourage Americans from gambling on the Internet through legislation aimed at gambling operators as well as at the financial institutions that mediate payments between operators and customers. However, it is unlikely that criminalization will eradicate Internet gambling. Furthermore, given the interest of many state and tribal governments as well as private operators in developing Internet gambling sites, it may be that this "Pandora's box" is already open.

PROBLEM GAMBLING AS A SOCIAL ISSUE

As noted above, the "third wave" of gambling legalization in the 1980s and 1990s was one of two important social and historical trends that intersected in the United States in the final quarter of the twentieth century. The second was changes in the American health care system that led to more frequent recognition by mental health professionals of a range of mental illnesses. The intersection of the "social worlds"[39] of gambling and psychiatry was key to both the rapid expansion of legal gambling in America and the public acceptance of problem gambling as a legitimate social problem.

The "medicalization" of problem gambling represents a convergence of the interests of the psychiatric profession and the problem gambling "community"—largely made up of recovering problem gamblers—in making treatment for gambling problems, among other social problems, more professional and more available. For the medical professions, defining problem gambling as a disease meant another disorder for whose treatment insurance companies and HMOs as well as individual clients could be persuaded to pay. For the recovering community, defining problem gambling as a disease held the promise of destigmatizing its sufferers, with simultaneous changes in how problem gamblers would be dealt with by the justice system as well as by families and friends.

The various editions of the *Diagnostic and Statistical Manual* (DSM) of the American Psychiatric Association are a reflection of major political and theoretical shifts that have occurred in American psychiatry in the twentieth century. The DSM is now an integral part of the modern mental health enterprise. The manual is widely used in judicial and educational decision-making as well as in decisions about reimbursement for health care and in the development of drugs by the pharmaceutical industry. The DSM impacts scientific research and higher education as well as governments' decisions about the allocation of public health funds.[40]

In the 1970s, third-party reimbursements for psychotherapy expanded rapidly, leading to expansion in the availability of outpatient treatment for mental health problems. In addition to the drive to capture more financial coverage for psychiatric treatment, the developers of the DSM-III, the third edition of the DSM, were motivated by the need to include an expanding array of conditions with which practitioners were confronted in outpatient settings and by their concern to maintain the reputation of psychiatry as a legitimate branch of medicine. In 1980, pathological gambling, along with Post-traumatic Stress Disorder and Borderline Personality Disorder, became one of the new conditions that psychiatrists and other mental health workers could officially identify.[41]

MOBILIZING THE PROBLEM GAMBLING COMMUNITY

In the 1950s and 1960s, in spite of the fact that many people gambled, most forms of gambling were illegal and gambling was widely viewed as morally suspect. Problem gamblers were seen as criminals—"degenerates" who "gambled out of control as a result of greed."[42] During this period, a small number of psychiatrists began to argue that at least some people with gambling problems were "sick" rather than "bad" and to suggest that the social institution best equipped to address this issue was medicine, rather than the criminal justice system.[43] While most medical and mental health professionals gave little credence to this argument, it was embraced by members of Gamblers Anonymous, a self-help group that started in California in the early 1950s.[44]

In the 1970s, Dr. Robert Custer, a psychiatrist in charge of a Veterans Administration addictions unit in Ohio, was approached by a local Gamblers Anonymous group for help with several of their members whose problems were particularly severe.[45] Custer was successful in establishing an inpatient treatment program for gamblers at the Brecksville Veterans Administration Medical Center and information from this program was instrumental in the initial inclusion of pathological gambling in the DSM in 1980. Also during the 1970s, a new national organization dedicated to raising public awareness about problem gambling was formed.[46] The National Council on Compulsive (later Problem) Gambling, made up largely of members of Gamblers Anonymous and Gam-Anon, as well as a few "influential citizens" including Custer and Monsignor Joseph Dunne of the New York City Police Department, was incorporated in 1975 and set out to educate health care providers and legislators about the need to define problem gamblers as suffering from "a psychologically uncontrollable illness."

During the 1980s and then, more rapidly, in the 1990s, a constituency of well-educated treatment professionals emerged whose livelihoods involve providing services related to problem gambling to governments and gambling operators. Organizations that support these helping professions—hospitals, clinics, government health agencies, universities and colleges, and the insurance industry—have growing interests in how legal gambling develops and in how problem gambling is defined. Though still relatively modest, these organizations are investing increasing resources in training and certifying treatment professionals, in educating students, and in covering treatment for pathological gambling. For varying reasons, many of these social institutions have adopted the view of problem gambling as a medical disorder.

GRUDGING ACCEPTANCE BY INDUSTRY AND GOVERNMENT

In the 1990s, the gambling industries and state governments embraced, albeit grudgingly, the notion of problem gambling as a medical disorder. From the perspective of the gambling industries, with the specter of Big Tobacco before them, accepting some responsibility for problem gambling and addressing the issue from within the industry is preferable to government regulation and the likelihood of additional taxation. Another element that led to a change in the posture of the gambling industries has been growing grassroots opposition to the expansion of gambling and the concomitant need for the gambling industries to appear socially responsible.

The gambling industries did not accept the medical definition of problem gambling with open arms. Within the industries, concerns about viewing problem gambling as a medical issue had to do with the difficulties attendant on collecting debts from problem gamblers and with questions of liability. The notion of problem gambling as a medical disorder was viewed by gambling operators as a way for problem gamblers to escape personal responsibility for their actions and, more importantly, for their gambling debts. Operators also believed that the medicalization of problem gambling allowed governments to escape any blame for the negative consequences flowing from gambling legalization by placing responsibility for problem gambling on the operators. They argued that this, in turn, would reduce the benefits gained by communities and governments from legalized gambling, such as tax revenues and jobs.

Although it was not a perfect fit, the view of problem gambling as a medical disorder solved a critical difficulty for the newly legitimate operators of casinos and lotteries in the United States. While significant strides had been made to change the image of these industries as "deviant" and "criminal," the gambling industries still faced challenges posed by public disapproval of individuals who got into trouble with their gambling. Defining problem gambling as a disease rather than as a moral issue gave the gambling industries a new framework within which to address this "negative externality" unique to their operations.

The challenge for governments has been their awkward position as both regulators and operators of gambling.[47] State governments are in the difficult position of promoting some types of gambling and prosecuting others. One consequence of the blurring of the boundaries between government and gambling has been a failure on the part of state governments—and the federal government—to address problem gambling in any organized fashion. This has left the field open for negotiations between the gambling industries on the one hand and the problem gambling treatment and research community on the other.

As Brian Castellani argues, our view of problem gambling at the beginning of the twenty-first century "is not a function of research and clinical investigation alone. There are political, institutional, professional and economic factors involved as well. Understanding how these 'non-clinical' and 'non-empirical' factors influence the way we think about pathological gambling is important."[48] Specifically, the particular social and historical conditions that have given rise to the emergence of problem gambling as a medical issue must not blind us to alternative ways in which problem gambling can be viewed and addressed by society.

4

WHAT IS THE EXTENT OF
PROBLEM GAMBLING?

This chapter examines the extent of problem and pathological gambling in the general population and in specific subgroups in the population. Given accumulating evidence that some types of gambling are more closely associated with the development of gambling-related problems than others, the chapter also examines the relationship between problem gambling and specific gambling activities. Consideration of the extent of problem gambling in the community must begin, however, with some understanding of how problem gambling is measured.

MEASURING PROBLEM GAMBLING

The tools used to generate numbers are always a reflection of the work that researchers and others are doing within larger social, political, and economic contexts.[1] Historically, standardized measures and indices often have emerged in situations where there is both intense distrust and a perceived need for public action. Examples include the emergence of measures of "public utility" in France in the mid-1800s and the development of cost-benefit analysis in the United States in the 1950s.[2]

With the rapid expansion of legal gambling in the 1980s and 1990s, state governments slowly began establishing services for individuals with gambling problems. In making decisions about funding such programs, policymakers quickly sought answers to questions about the number of individuals in the general population who might seek help for their gambling difficulties. These questions required epidemiological research to identify the number (or "cases") of problem and pathological gamblers, to ascertain the demographic characteristics of these individuals, and to determine the likelihood that they would utilize treatment services if these became available.

Following inclusion of pathological gambling in the third edition of the *Diagnostic and Statistical Manual* (DSM-III) in 1980, a few researchers began to investigate problem gambling using methods from psychiatric epidemiology. At that time, few tools existed to measure gambling-related difficulties. The only tool rigorously developed and tested for its performance was the South Oaks Gambling Screen (SOGS). Closely based on the new diagnostic criteria, the SOGS was originally developed to screen for gambling problems in clinical populations.[3]

Like other tools in psychiatric research, the SOGS was quickly adapted for use in epidemiological research. The SOGS was first used in a prevalence survey in New York State.[4] By 1999, the SOGS—in one or another of its various forms—had been used in population-based research in more than forty-five jurisdictions in the United States, Canada, Asia, and Europe.[5] This widespread use was due, at least in part, to the comparability within and across jurisdictions that came with use of a standard tool.[6] Although there were increasingly well-focused grounds for concern about the performance of the SOGS in nonclinical environments, this tool remained the de facto standard in the field until the mid-1990s, when new criteria were published in the fourth edition of the DSM (DSM-IV).[7]

HOW WELL DO OUR TOOLS WORK?

Like all tools to detect physical and psychological maladies, screens to detect gambling problems make errors in classification. However, misclassification has very different consequences in different settings. While most screens to detect psychiatric disorders work well in clinical settings where the prevalence of such disorders is predictably high, their accuracy declines when used among populations where prevalence is much lower.[8] In general population research, where base rates of most psychiatric disorders are extremely low, most clinically derived tools generate substantial numbers of "false positives." While this has the potential to inflate estimated prevalence rates significantly, "false negatives" also tend to increase and may entirely counteract the effect of a high rate of false positives. In population research, where the primary concern is accurately identifying the number of people with and without the disorder, both types of classification error are important since each has an independent impact on the overall efficiency of the screen. Indeed, the rate of false negatives may be of principal concern in population research since even a very low rate of false negatives can have a large effect on the overall efficiency of a screen (that is, the total proportion of individuals who are correctly classified).

A national study in New Zealand in the early 1990s furnished an opportunity to examine the performance of a slightly revised version of the South Oaks Gambling Screen, dubbed the SOGS-R, in the general population.[9] The New Zealand research team found that the *lifetime* screen is actually quite good at detecting pathological gambling among those who *currently* experience the disorder. As expected, however, the lifetime screen identifies at-risk individuals at the expense of generating a substantial number of false positives. The *current* screen produces fewer false positives than the lifetime measure but more false negatives and thus provides a weaker screen for identifying pathological gamblers in the clinical sense. However, the greater *efficiency* of the current screen makes it a more useful tool for detecting rates of change in the prevalence of problem and pathological gambling over time. A recent study in Minnesota supported the New Zealand work on the performance of the SOGS-R in different subgroups in the population.[10]

THE EMERGENCE OF NEW TOOLS

Beginning in the early 1990s, a variety of methodological questions were raised about SOGS-based research in the general population. Some of these issues, such as respondent denial and rising refusal rates, were common to all survey research.[11] Other questions were related to the issue of how to best study gambling problems.[12] These included reservations about the performance of the SOGS in population studies as well as challenges to assumptions about the nature of problem gambling that were built into the original version of this instrument.

What led to the growing dissatisfaction with the South Oaks Gambling Screen? One important change was the rapid expansion of legal gambling itself. As legal gambling expanded and as new groups began to gamble, more women, minorities, and middle-class individuals experienced gambling-related difficulties and the people seeking help became increasingly heterogeneous.[13] Representatives of the lottery and casino industries also played a role in challenging the supremacy of the SOGS through their efforts to discredit what they saw as unacceptably high prevalence rates. Another reason for dissatisfaction grew from the multiplying need for tools to identify problem gamblers in different settings. As government resources for problem gambling services increased, demands for accountability and performance rose and drew further attention to the deficiencies of the SOGS.

In spite of challenges, the SOGS remained the major tool to identify individuals with gambling problems in clinical settings and in survey research throughout the 1990s. However, since the publication of the DSM-IV in 1994 with a revised set of criteria for pathological gambling, a multitude of new problem gambling screens for adults and for adolescents have been developed.[14] Despite this proliferation, the psychometric properties of most of these new tools, as well as their differential performance in various settings, remain unexamined.[15] Another concern is how to calibrate the performance of these new screens with the results of more than a decade of SOGS-based research. While research suggests that scores on several of the new problem gambling screens and the SOGS are highly correlated and are probably measures of the same underlying construct,[16] there is still much work to be done in this area.

The assumption underlying all of the existing gambling research is that gambling-related difficulties are a robust phenomenon and that these difficulties can be measured. Despite agreement among researchers and treatment professionals at this fundamental level, there is disagreement about how to conceptualize and measure gambling-related difficulties. Although the presence of competing concepts and methods is not uncommon in many scientific fields, disputes among experts have led to some degree of public confusion and uncertainty about the impacts of legal gambling on society.

Like much of science, measurement tools are a reflection of the work that researchers are doing to identify and describe the phenomena that interest them. As research on problem gambling continues, our tools for identifying problem gamblers can be expected to change. The SOGS represents a culturally and historically situated consensus about the nature of problem gambling. As research continues and as the definitions of problem gambling change, new instruments and new methods for estimating prevalence in the general population and for testing models of gambling behavior will continue to emerge. These emerging methods must be tested against one another and against the SOGS in order to advance the field of problem gambling research in an orderly manner, ensuring the relevance of our past work as well as our work in the future.

PROBLEM GAMBLING IN THE GENERAL POPULATION

Until 1998, only one national prevalence survey had been conducted in the United States.[17] Although the screen used to measure "compulsive" gambling in this survey has been criticized,[18] it provided the first-ever prevalence estimates of this disorder. The overall prevalence of "probable compulsive gambling" was deemed to be 0.77 percent (1.1 percent for men, 0.5 percent for women). A further 2.3 percent of the respondents were classified as "potential compulsive gamblers." In Nevada, which was oversampled because of the researchers' interest in comparing states with and without casino gambling, the prevalence of "probable compulsive gambling" was much higher than the national average, namely 2.5 percent (3.3 percent for men, 2.0 percent for women). Based largely on the strong relationship between the availability of gambling and gambling participation and the differences between Nevada and the rest of the country, the researchers concluded that widespread legalization of gambling in the United States was likely to result in a significant increase in problem gambling.

In 1998, the National Gambling Impact Study Commission initiated an extensive research program as part of its charge to conduct "a comprehensive study of the social and economic impacts of gambling in the United States."[19] The national Gambling Impact and Behavior Study—or GIBS—was one of several elements in the full program of research. The GIBS, carried out by the National Opinion Research Center and its partners, included five separate initiatives: a nationally representative telephone survey of 2,417 adults; a national telephone survey of 534 youths ages sixteen and seventeen; intercept interviews with 530 adult patrons of gaming facilities; a longitudinal database (1980 to 1997) of social and economic indicators, including gambling revenues, in a random national sample of one hundred communities; and case studies in ten communities of the effects of large-scale casinos opening in close proximity.[20]

Guidelines from the National Gambling Impact Study Commission specified that the DSM-IV criteria were to be used to identify problem and pathological gamblers in the general population. This meant that none of the existing versions of the SOGS could be used since that instrument is based on the original, DSM-III, criteria. In constructing the questionnaire for the adult, youth, and patron surveys, the national research team developed a new problem gambling screen. The NORC Diagnostic Screen for Gambling Problems (NODS) was tested for its performance in a clinical sample prior to its adoption in the national surveys. In these tests, the screen demonstrated strong internal consistency, high sensitivity, and good specificity and retest reliability. Unfortunately, since there is no information about how the performance of the NODS compares with the problem gambling screen used in the first national survey, in 1975, there is no way to compare problem gambling prevalence rates in 1975 and 1998.

Results based on the lifetime NODS and the combined samples of adults and gaming facility patrons showed that the national prevalence of "pathological gambling" (NODS ≥ 5) was 1.2 percent (1.7 percent for men, 0.8 percent for women). A further 1.5 percent of the respondents in the combined sample were classified as "problem gamblers" (NODS = 3 or 4). Based on these figures, the research team estimated that about 2.5 million American adults are pathological gamblers and another 3 million adults should be considered problem gamblers. Extending the criteria more broadly, an additional 7.7 percent of the respondents were classified as "at risk" (NODS = 1 or 2). This represents about 15 million American adults who can be considered at risk for problem gambling.

Based on the combined sample of adults and gaming facility patrons, the national research team found that men are more likely to be pathological, problem, or at-risk gamblers than women; that pathological, problem, and at-risk gambling are more common among African Americans than among other ethnic groups; that about one in five of the 1 percent of adults who consider themselves professional gamblers can be classified as "pathological"; and that the availability of a casino within 50 miles (versus 50 to 250 miles) is associated with about double the prevalence of problem and pathological gambling.

CHANGES IN PROBLEM GAMBLING OVER TIME

Compared to the two national studies, which were conducted twenty-five years apart, there is a great deal more information about changes in the prevalence of problem gambling from the numerous state- and province-level surveys that have been conducted in North America since 1975. These include a recent meta-analysis conducted by a team of Harvard researchers, as well as the results of a growing number of problem gambling replication surveys conducted throughout North America. Taken together, these data suggest that the prevalence of problem and pathological gambling has increased in North America, particularly since 1993. While it is difficult to identify statistically significant changes when prevalence surveys are carried out too closely together, the data do indicate that the *severity* of problem gambling is increasing, as the proportion of individuals who score at the higher end of the problem gambling continuum is growing.

The Harvard meta-analysis of 120 North American problem gambling prevalence studies obtained a mean current—or past-year—prevalence rate of probable pathological gambling of 1.14 percent (±0.24) and a mean current problem gambling prevalence rate of 2.80 percent (±0.85). When the researchers compared the average prevalence rate among surveys conducted from 1975 to 1993 with the average prevalence rate among surveys conducted between 1994 and 1996, they found that the combined prevalence of problem and probable pathological gambling was significantly higher in the later studies (6.72 percent compared with 4.38 percent). The researchers also found that past-year rates of probable pathological gambling averaged 0.84 percent for surveys carried out between 1975 and 1993 and 1.29 percent for those carried out between 1994 and 1996. As with the lifetime rates, this difference was statistically significant.[21]

While results averaged over a large number of studies can be informative, it is often more helpful to examine data from states and provinces where surveys of problem gambling have been replicated. There are now a growing number of North American jurisdictions where *replication* surveys of problem and pathological gambling have been carried out. Three of these studies, in Iowa, Quebec, and New York, were only able to measure changes in lifetime prevalence.[22] All three of these studies, conducted six years, seven years, and ten years, respectively, after the baseline studies, identified significant increases in the lifetime prevalence of problem and probable pathological gambling.[23]

We noted above that the lifetime South Oaks Gambling Screen is very good at detecting gambling problems among those who currently experience the disorder. The current screen is a less effective clinical tool, but its greater overall efficiency makes it more useful for detecting rates of change in the prevalence of problem gambling over time. There are now thirteen North American jurisdictions that have funded replication studies to assess changes in the current prevalence of problem and probable pathological gambling.[24] Table 4.1 presents information on the prevalence of past-year problem and probable pathological gambling at baseline and at replication in jurisdictions where current prevalence data were collected at both times. The jurisdictions appear in order of the interval of time between the baseline and the replication study and the year in which the baseline study was done.

From Table 4.1 it is evident that very little change is found in jurisdictions where replication studies are done within two years of the baseline study (that is, Manitoba, Michigan, and South Dakota). In the six North American jurisdictions where replication studies were completed three years after the baseline, the overall prevalence of problem gambling declined in four jurisdictions (Louisiana, Oregon, Alberta, and New Brunswick), and increased in British Columbia and Texas. In jurisdictions where replication studies were completed four or more years after the baseline study, the overall prevalence of problem gambling declined in Washington State, remained stable in North Dakota, and increased in Minnesota and Montana. While the data are interesting, no trends are apparent in these changes in problem gambling prevalence rates over different periods of time in different jurisdictions.

A more illuminating approach to these data is to examine differences in the *magnitude* of changes across these jurisdictions. Figure 4.1 (page 55) presents information about the magnitude of changes in current problem gambling prevalence across several states where replication surveys recently have been conducted. In interpreting Figure 4.1, it is important to note that these are not differences in the prevalence rates between baseline and replication, but rather the magnitude of such differences.[25] As in Table 4.1, the jurisdictions are arranged according to the interval between the two studies and the year when the first study was done.

TABLE 4.1. NORTH AMERICAN CURRENT PROBLEM AND PROBABLE PATHOLOGICAL GAMBLING PREVALENCE RATES AT BASELINE AND REPLICATION AFTER TWO, THREE, FOUR, OR MORE YEARS

	JURISDICTION	CURRENT PROBLEM (%)	CURRENT PROBABLE PATHOLOGICAL (%)	CURRENT TOTAL (%)
TWO YEARS				
1991	South Dakota	0.8	0.6	1.4
1993	South Dakota	0.7	0.5	1.2
1993	Manitoba	2.9	1.3	4.2
1995	Manitoba	2.4	1.9	4.3
1997	Michigan	2.1	1.3	3.4
1999	Michigan	2.0	1.2	3.2
THREE YEARS				
1992	Texas	1.7	0.8	2.5
1995	Texas	2.2	0.8	3.0
1992	New Brunswick	3.1	1.4	4.5
1995	New Brunswick	1.9	2.2	4.1
1993	British Columbia	2.4	1.1	3.5
1996	British Columbia	2.8	1.1	3.9
1994	Alberta	4.0	1.4	5.4
1997	Alberta	2.8	2.0	4.8
1995	Louisiana	3.4	1.4	4.8
1998	Louisiana	2.3	1.6	3.9
1997	Oregon	1.9	1.4	3.3
2000	Oregon	1.4	0.9	2.3
FOUR OR MORE YEARS				
1990	Minnesota	1.6	0.9	2.5
1994	Minnesota	3.2	1.2	4.4
1992	Montana	1.5	0.7	2.2
1998	Montana	1.9	1.3	3.2

cont. on next page

TABLE 4.1. NORTH AMERICAN CURRENT PROBLEM AND
PROBABLE PATHOLOGICAL GAMBLING PREVALENCE
RATES AT BASELINE AND REPLICATION AFTER
TWO, THREE, AND FOUR OR MORE YEARS, CONT.

JURISDICTION		CURRENT PROBLEM (%)	CURRENT PROBABLE PATHOLOGICAL (%)	CURRENT TOTAL (%)
FOUR OR MORE YEARS				
1992	Washington State	1.9	0.9	2.8
1998	Washington State	1.8	0.5	2.3
1992	North Dakota	1.3	0.7	2.0
2000	North Dakota	0.7	1.4	2.1

Sources: Max W. Abbott and Rachel A. Volberg, *Gambling and Problem Gambling in the Community: An International Overview and Critique* (Wellington: New Zealand Department of Internal Affairs, 1999); Rachel A. Volberg, *Gambling and Problem Gambling in North Dakota: A Replication Study, 1992 to 2000* (Bismarck, N.D.: Office of the Governor, 2001); Rachel A. Volberg, *Changes in Gambling and Problem Gambling in Oregon, 1997 to 2000,* report to the Oregon Gambling Addiction Treatment Foundation (Salem: Oregon Gambling Addiction Treatment Foundation, 2001); Rachel A. Volberg and Walton L. Moore, "Gambling and Problem Gambling in Louisiana: A Replication Study, 1995 to 1998," Appendix D, in Timothy P. Ryan and Janet F. Speyrer, *Gambling in Louisiana: A Benefit/Cost Analysis,* report to the Louisiana Gaming Control Board (New Orleans: University of New Orleans, 1999).

Figure 4.1 shows that, while combined prevalence rates may not change appreciably in short periods of time, there can be substantial changes in the prevalence of probable pathological gambling over time and, therefore, in the proportion of individuals within the group of problem gamblers who are experiencing more severe difficulties. Similar changes have been identified in several Canadian provinces, including Alberta, Manitoba, and New Brunswick.[26]

If we accept a change in magnitude of 15 percent as significant,[27] Figure 4.1 shows that the combined current prevalence of problem and probable pathological gambling (as measured by the South Oaks Gambling Screen) declined in three of the five jurisdictions under consideration (Louisiana, Oregon, and Washington State), remained stable in North Dakota, and increased in Montana. In contrast, the current prevalence of probable pathological gambling *alone*—that is, the group of respondents at the most severe end of the problem gambling continuum—increased substantially in both Montana and North Dakota, remained stable in Louisiana, and declined in Oregon and Washington State.

FIGURE 4.1. CHANGES IN PROBLEM GAMBLING PREVALENCE ACROSS SELECTED U.S. JURISDICTIONS

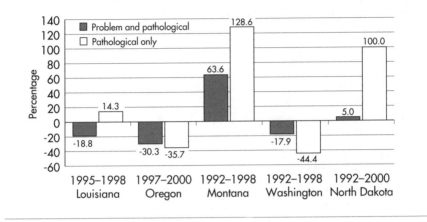

Source: Rachel A. Volberg, *Changes in Gambling and Problem Gambling in Oregon, 1997 to 2000*, report to the Oregon Gambling Addiction Treatment Foundation (Salem: Oregon Gambling Addiction Treatment Foundation, 2001).

It is worth noting that in the two jurisdictions where prevalence rates declined—Oregon and Washington State—as well as in Louisiana, where the prevalence rate was stable, there were relatively strong problem gambling service systems in place during the period between the baseline and replication surveys. In contrast, in the period between the baseline and replication surveys in Montana and North Dakota, there were almost no services available for problem gamblers and their families.

A degree of caution is necessary in interpreting these data due to the relatively small sample sizes and complex sampling designs used in all of these studies. However, the consistency of these changes over a considerable period of time as well as across a variety of jurisdictions suggests that these are reliable trends rather than the result of sampling error.

WHO IS AT RISK FOR PROBLEM GAMBLING?

In an extensive review of the problem gambling literature, the National Research Council concluded that, while past studies have provided a solid foundation, more and better research is needed on the specific risk factors that lead to either the initiation of gambling or to progression from nonproblematic to problem or pathological gambling. The National Research Council also called for research that considers which factors for chronic, long-term gambling are unique and not simply predictors of excessive behavior in general.

In spite of these caveats, there is a substantial amount of information available about the risk factors associated with problem gambling. The authors of the Harvard meta-analysis identified several risk factors associated with higher rates of what they called "disordered" gambling. They concluded that those most at risk for gambling-related problems are:

> (1) indifferent or insensitive to the social pressures or sanctions against immoderate behavior (e.g. the social separation often experienced by people with major mental illness, or the new independence commonly experienced by college students), (2) extremely sensitive to the perceived social pressures to participate in activities that they consider normative (e.g. as a result of the peer pressure often experienced by adolescents), or (3) in physical or emotional discomfort that is ameliorated by the gambling experience (e.g. people who are depressed and find that gambling relieves their discomfort).

As a result, the Harvard researchers argued, "being young, male, in college, having psychiatric co-morbidity, or a history of anti-social behavior are factors that represent meaningful risks for developing gambling-related problems."[28]

Recent surveys in New Zealand and Sweden suggest that those most at risk for gambling problems are the groups most disadvantaged and marginalized by changes occurring in national and international economies worldwide: young, unemployed, male members of ethnic minorities.[29] The results of several other studies, including recent prevalence surveys in Louisiana, Montana, and Oregon, as well as the national survey in Australia, suggest that gambling problems are increasingly likely to affect women.[30]

Additional information about changes in the characteristics of problem gamblers over time comes from several recent replication surveys. Like gambling participation and problem gambling prevalence rates, changes in the characteristics of problem gamblers in different jurisdictions exhibit different patterns. In Louisiana, problem gamblers in 1998 were significantly more likely than those in 1995 to be women and to be between the ages of thirty-five and fifty-four.[31] In Oregon, problem gamblers in 2000 were more likely than those in 1997 to be female and to be Native American and were significantly more likely to have graduated from college and to have annual household incomes over $50,000.[32] In Montana, as in Oregon, problem gamblers in 1998 were still just as likely as problem gamblers in 1992 to be women but were significantly more likely to be Native American.[33] In Washington State, problem gamblers in 1998 were significantly more likely than those in 1992 to be male, to be non-white, and to have graduated from high school.[34] In North Dakota, problem gamblers in 2000 were significantly more likely than those in 1992 to be male and to be Native American.[35]

Differences in gender and age explain much of the variation in gambling participation across the United States.[36] As I pointed out earlier in this report, gambling activities take place in a wide variety of settings and appeal to different groups of people. It is possible that the high proportion of problem gamblers in Louisiana, Montana, and Oregon who are women is the result of widespread availability in these states of electronic gaming devices at venues that did not previously offer gambling. It is also possible that the growing proportion of problem gamblers in North Dakota and Washington State who are minority men is the result of the introduction of Native American casino gambling and card rooms in these states. These are hypotheses, however, that remain to be tested as the monitoring of gambling and problem gambling prevalence continues in these jurisdictions.

PROBLEM GAMBLING AND SPECIFIC GAMBLING ACTIVITIES

Until recently, little notice was taken by gambling researchers or policymakers of particular features of different gambling activities and their likely impact on the prevalence of problem gambling in the general population. While gambling activities can be classified in many ways, several researchers have suggested that *event frequency*, or the number of opportunities to wager in a specified period of time, is closely related to the development of gambling problems.[37] Another critical concern is the spread of "convenience gambling" outside of venues traditionally reserved for gambling. Convenience gambling was defined by the National Gambling Impact Study Commission as "legal, stand-alone slot machines, video poker, video keno and other EGDs [electronic gaming devices] that have proliferated in bars, truck stops, convenience stores and a variety of other locations."[38]

While there has been little analysis, there are data available that are relevant to the relationship between specific types of gambling and/or features of gambling games and the prevalence of problem gambling. The recent Australian national survey is particularly important in this context because of the widespread availability of gaming machines in Australia.[39] Gaming machines in Australia, known as "pokies," are stand-alone machines with keys or touch-sensitive screens that accept coins or bills and offer video poker, video keno, video bingo, and video blackjack as well as traditional "reel" games of the kind offered on casino slot machines. There are thousands of gaming machines located at social clubs, hotels, bars, and restaurants in most of the Australian states. Looking across the different states, the Australian researchers found that as the number of machines per capita increased, both the proportion of the adult population that played weekly and the proportion of problem gamblers among weekly players increased.

Findings from recent state-level studies in Louisiana, Montana, New York, and Oregon support the conclusion that greater numbers of machines are associated with higher problem gambling prevalence rates. To place these data in context, Table 4.2 presents information on the salient features of EGDs in these four states.[40] The table shows that Montana authorized EGDs much earlier than any of the other states. While the EGDs in New York and Oregon are owned and operated by the state lottery, the EGDs in Louisiana and Montana are regulated by the state but are privately owned and operated. While Louisiana and Oregon have less than one video poker machine per capita, Montana has more than five machines per capita.

There are other features of these games that are important for understanding differences in participation and problem gambling prevalence rates. While keno drawings are broadcast on a single screen that players can watch after purchasing a ticket, video poker is played on stand-alone machines, with keys or a touch-sensitive screen, into which players feed coins (or bills) directly. Although keno is most often played at bars or restaurants, it is also available in other, more traditional lottery outlets, such as convenience stores. In contrast, video poker is closely linked to licenses to sell and/or serve alcoholic beverages. Since conditions for obtaining such licenses vary across

TABLE 4.2. FEATURES OF ELECTRONIC GAMING
DEVICES IN SELECTED STATES

	MONTANA		OREGON		LOUISIANA	NEW YORK
	KENO	VIDEO POKER	KENO	VIDEO POKER	VIDEO POKER	KENO
Year authorized	1976	1985	1991	1992	1992	1995
Ownership		Private	State	State	Private	State
Maximum payout		$800	$1,000,000	$600	$500	$100,000
Number of locations		1,740	≈2,000	1,854	≈3,600	≈3,200
Reported number of machines		17,397		8,848	15,000	—
Number of machines per outlet		Up to 20	1 monitor	Up to 20	Variable	1 monitor
Tied to liquor license		Yes	No	Yes	Yes	No
Game frequency		15 seconds	5 minutes	15 seconds	15 seconds	5 minutes
Past-year play		39%	—	24%	19%	17%
Weekly play		9%	1%	3%	3%	3%

Source: Rachel A. Volberg, *Quick Draw Players in New York State: A Comparison of Data from 1996 and 1999* (Albany: New York State Office of Mental Health, 2000), Table 13, p. 20; National Gambling Impact Study Commission, *Final Report* (Washington, D.C.: U.S. Government Printing Office, 1999), Table 2-1, p. 2-4.

states, EGDs may be located in a variety of settings, including bars, restaurants, hotels, truck stops, racetracks, and off-track betting facilities. A final contrast between video keno and other EGDs is in the frequency of the game. Keno provides a new game every five minutes, whereas a hand of video poker can be played in about fifteen seconds.

In the states studied, higher past-year and weekly participation rates are associated with higher numbers of machines per capita as well as with event frequency. Table 4.2 shows that in New York and Oregon, only 1 to 3 percent of adults play the slower keno game on a weekly basis. In Louisiana and Oregon, the faster video poker game (on stand-alone machines) is associated with higher rates of past-year participation (19 percent in Louisiana and 24 percent in Oregon), although, as with keno, only about 3 percent of the adult population participates in video poker one or more times a week. In Montana, where several video gambling games are available on far more numerous stand-alone machines, 39 percent of the adult population has played on these machines in the past year, and 9 percent play these machines once a week or more often.

Table 4.3 shows problem gambling prevalence rates among weekly EGD players and other weekly gamblers in all of these states. These prevalence rates are based on the Fisher DSM-IV Screen (which provides only a past-year measure of problem gambling) rather than the more widely used South Oaks Gambling Screen. While the small sample sizes indicate that caution is necessary in interpreting these results, the table shows that the prevalence of problem gambling among EGD players is substantially higher than among other weekly gamblers. The table also shows that problem gambling prevalence rates are higher in Louisiana and Oregon, where video poker has been operating for less than a decade, than in Montana, where gaming machines have been operating for substantially longer, or in New York, where only the slower keno game is available.

The potential link between the availability of specific types of gambling and problem gambling prevalence is a critical policy issue. While causation is difficult to prove without longitudinal research, there is a correlation between the availability of EGDs and higher prevalence rates of problem gambling, particularly among women. These links should be a matter of concern to policymakers at all levels of government as they make decisions related to legal gambling in their jurisdictions.

TABLE 4.3. PROBLEM GAMBLING PREVALENCE AMONG WEEKLY
EGD PLAYERS AND OTHER WEEKLY GAMBLERS

	GAMBLING ACTIVITY (WEEKLY)	GROUP SIZE	PROBLEM (3 TO 4 POINTS)	CONFIDENCE INTERVAL	PROBABLE/ PATHOLOGICAL (5+ POINTS)	CONFIDENCE INTERVAL	TOTAL PREVALENCE	CONFIDENCE INTERVAL
New York	Keno (1999)	500	7.9	±2.4	4.0	±1.7	11.9	±2.8
	Other (1996)	593	2.7	±1.3	2.3	±1.2	5.0	±1.7
Oregon	Video poker	42	14.3	±12.6	23.8	±12.6	38.1	±14.7
	Other	215	6.5	±3.3	1.4	±1.6	7.9	±3.6
Montana	Video gaming machine	108	7.4	±4.9	7.4	±4.9	14.8	±6.7
	Other	124	2.4	±2.7	1.6	±2.2	4.0	±3.4
Louisiana	Video poker	61	9.8	±7.5	11.5	±8.0	21.3	±10.3
	Other	306	5.6	±2.6	1.3	±1.3	6.9	±2.8

Source: Rachel A. Volberg, *Quick Draw Players in New York State: A Comparison of Data from 1996 and 1999* (Albany: New York State Office of Mental Health, 2000), Tables 14 and 15, pp. 22–23.

WHERE WILL PREVALENCE RATES GO FROM HERE?

While research shows that the prevalence of problem gambling has increased significantly in the United States, particularly since 1993, a critical question for policymakers is: will these prevalence rates continue to rise? In the early 1990s, as prevalence rates in state-level studies rose, researchers believed that they were seeing the early consequences of a rapid expansion in gambling availability and participation. Previous research, indicating that gambling problems usually take many years to develop, suggested that problem gambling prevalence rates would continue to increase in the future, particularly as gambling participation grew within sectors of the population that had previously gambled little, if at all. However, prevalence is not only a function of the rate of new cases (or "inflow"). Rather, the prevalence rate at any point in time also is determined by the duration of the disorder. Duration influences what can be thought of as the "outflow" that takes place through self-recovery, successful treatment, emigration, or death.

Pathological gambling is generally regarded as a chronic, or chronically relapsing, condition for the majority of people who develop gambling problems. Research with individuals in professional treatment programs and in self-help groups has supported this.[41] However, a recent study in New Zealand, which constitutes the first prospective community study of problem gambling, contradicts this psychiatric conceptualization, as well as clinical lore and the findings of earlier studies.[42] The New Zealand researchers found that while one-third of the problem and pathological gamblers had either remained problematic or developed more serious problems when reassessed seven years later, two-thirds of the group scored as nonproblematic. Even at the most severe end of the continuum, three-quarters of the probable pathological gamblers were nonproblematic seven years after their initial assessment. These findings suggest that problem gambling displays less chronicity than is generally believed to be the case. The study also found that the worst prognosis was for individuals with the most severe problems and for those who had co-morbid alcohol-related problems.

The results of this study suggest that the "outflow" rate for problem and pathological gambling is much higher than researchers have assumed. Information from a variety of other sources in New Zealand suggests that there also may have been reductions in "inflow" from some groups previously found to be at very high risk for gambling problems (for example, young people, unemployed people, and those outside the paid workforce).

These findings, as well as the results of several recent replication surveys in the United States, lend credence to the scenario described by the Harvard researchers. Their meta-analysis drew attention to lessons learned about marijuana and hallucinogen users from the 1960s and 1970s. The authors noted that, like early drug users in the 1960s, "gamblers who first tested opportunities to gamble legally were different from those who began to gamble only when playing these games was sufficiently widespread that it was normative."[43] In a later paper, the same researchers suggest that, on the basis of social learning models, "while it is possible that the prevalence of these problems will continue to increase in the near future, it is also possible that it will remain constant or even begin to diminish."[44]

While this may be the case, the most recent data suggest that a distillation process is taking place, whereby the proportion of problem gamblers who are most seriously troubled and most difficult to treat is growing. Monitoring of gambling involvement and problem gambling prevalence rates will be needed in the future to assess changes in the prevalence of problem gambling and in the characteristics of problem gamblers in the community. It also will be important to assess the effectiveness of available services for problem gamblers and refine these to match services better with the individuals seeking help.

5

ADDRESSING
PROBLEM GAMBLING

In spite of the possibility that problem gambling rates may stabilize or even diminish over time, the need remains for a wide-ranging, rational public policy with regard to problem gambling. There is also a need for a broad array of services that can help minimize this unique negative externality of legal gambling. This chapter examines the development of an array of services for problem gamblers in the United States.

Services that have become available for problem gamblers in the United States fall into several broad areas, including (1) public awareness and prevention, (2) treatment, and (3) research. Organizations in both the public and private sectors have increased their efforts to address problem gambling in recent years, particularly since the passage of the National Gambling Impact Study Commission Act in 1996. While there is growing willingness in both the public and private sectors to address problem gambling, neither the level of interest nor the funds available for problem gambling programs have kept pace with the increases in revenues generated by legal gambling or with the availability of opportunities to gamble.

PUBLIC AWARENESS AND PREVENTION

Until the 1990s, public awareness of problem gambling was limited. Although the media have reported on a range of different gambling issues, this coverage tends either to trumpet the success of new casino and lottery operations in various states or to relate the sad, personal stories of people like Pete Rose, the baseball player caught gambling on sports, Leonard Tose, the former owner of the Philadelphia Eagles who lost a fortune in the Atlantic City casinos, or Art Schlichter, the former professional football player.[1]

In this environment, the National Council on Problem Gambling (NCPG) became a key player in the struggle to raise public awareness of problem gambling. Originally organized in the early 1970s by a small group of recovering gamblers, the NCPG has grown into a large and eclectic group whose members include psychiatrists, psychologists, social workers, researchers, recovering gamblers, family members, gaming company executives, and church leaders. A not-for-profit organization, NCPG engages in a variety of activities, including operation of a national help line, sponsorship of the *Journal of Gambling Studies,* national and regional conferences and training symposia, and administration of a national counselor certification program.

During the 1980s and 1990s, the network of state affiliates of the NCPG grew exponentially. In 1989, there were only eight state affiliates; by 2000, there were state affiliates in thirty-three states as well as several international associates. While some affiliates have paid staff and provide an array of services to problem gamblers in their states, most are volunteer operations with few sources of funding. None of the affiliates offer treatment, although many maintain lists of qualified treatment professionals for referral. Figure 5.1 provides information on the states where NCPG affiliates are active.

Perhaps because of the greater stigma historically attached to casino gambling, the casino industry has been the most proactive sector of the gambling industries in addressing the issue of problem gambling. The industry standard was set by Harrah's Entertainment, which, during the 1990s, developed separate programs, Bet Smart® and Project 21®, to address problem and underage gambling.

The American Gaming Association, headed by Frank Fahrenkopf, a lawyer and former chairman of the Republican National Committee, is another key industry organization active in raising awareness of problem gambling. The American Gaming Association has developed industrywide programs to address what it calls "disordered" gambling as well as underage gambling. The association's two most prominent programs are the annual "Responsible Gaming Education Week," which seeks to educate casino employees and the public about

FIGURE 5.1. PROBLEM GAMBLING SERVICES IN THE UNITED STATES

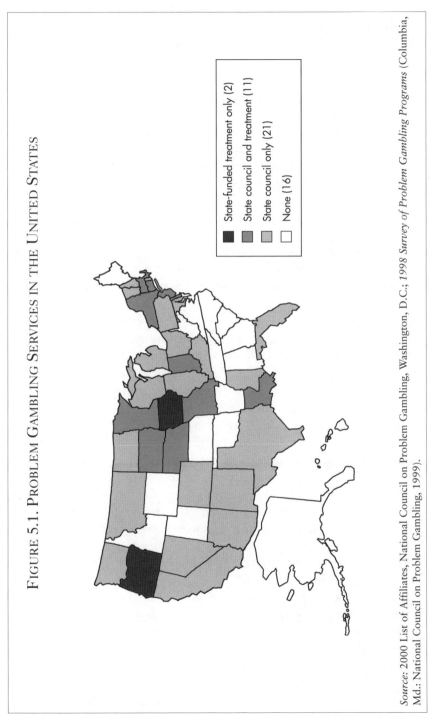

State-funded treatment only (2)

State council and treatment (11)

State council only (21)

None (16)

Source: 2000 List of Affiliates, National Council on Problem Gambling, Washington, D.C.; *1998 Survey of Problem Gambling Programs* (Columbia, Md.: National Council on Problem Gambling, 1999).

problem and underage gambling, and the National Center for Responsible Gaming, which funds peer-reviewed research on problem and underage gambling.[2]

The American Gaming Association has undertaken several other problem and underage gambling awareness and education initiatives. These include publication of a "Responsible Gaming Resource Guide" for casino companies; a multimedia, responsible gaming tool kit; sponsorship of a certification course for casino employees to learn how to respond to problem and underage gambling; development of an underage gambling training curriculum; and a partnership with the National Center for Missing and Exploited Children to ensure children's safety when visiting hotel-casino properties with their parents.

The "Responsible Gaming Resource Guide" describes a variety of strategies, policies, and procedures that can be adopted by casino companies wishing to address problem and/or underage gambling issues. Strategies for problem gambling include development of organizational mission statements and explicit codes of conduct for employees, establishment of clear responsibility within the organization for problem gambling initiatives, training for employee assistance professionals and supervisory staff to recognize gambling problems among industry employees and customers, suggestions for obtaining insurance coverage for industry employees with gambling problems, training for employees in awareness of problem gambling and in educating customers about the issue, establishment of policies regarding self-exclusion and the availability of credit, and partnerships with community agencies working with problem gamblers. Strategies to address underage gambling include orientation and training programs for employees, materials to educate customers about underage gambling, programs to heighten community awareness such as scholarships for local students who compete to develop anti-underage gambling materials, and enforcement of statutes related to underage gambling at casinos.[3]

Like the American Gaming Association at the national level, casino trade associations at the state level have been active in supporting problem gambling programs and in raising public awareness of problem gambling. In Illinois and Missouri, for example, the riverboat gaming associations, rather than the state governments, are the primary source of funding for problem gambling programs. Similar organizations of casino operators in Colorado, Louisiana, and Mississippi have been vocal and visible in support of problem gambling programs. In North Dakota, the North Dakota and Great Plains Indian Gaming Association is an important source of funds for problem gambling services. In fiscal year 2000, this organization provided major support for a problem gambling replication survey as well as for the statewide help line for problem gamblers.

Partly because lotteries are seen as a less harmful, "softer" form of gambling and partly because they are operated by state governments, pressures to respond to the problem gambling issue have been less intense for the lottery industry than for the casino industry. As a consequence, lotteries have been less active than the casino industry in working to raise public awareness of problem gambling. However, a growing number of state governments have mandated links between lotteries and problem gambling programs by redirecting a portion of lottery revenues or of a lottery's advertising budget to problem gambling programs. Several states require that all lottery tickets, lottery machines, and point-of-sale materials display a problem gambling help-line number.

Most of the problem gambling programs funded by state governments engage primarily in public awareness activities. A few states also have funded prevention activities, most notably Minnesota, where prevention programs focus on specific at-risk populations, including youths, the elderly, and people in substance abuse treatment programs. In its final report, the National Gambling Impact Study Commission cited testimony from the director of the Minnesota prevention programs and noted that these measures "seem to be having a positive impact."[4] In Connecticut, the Connecticut Council on Problem Gambling emphasizes prevention issues in a monthly newsletter that is distributed to problem gambling clinicians and researchers around the country. For the most part, however, problem gambling programs do not separate prevention from other activities in which they engage, particularly public education and awareness.

Researchers have noted that, with regard to a range of mental and physical disorders, "the preponderance of social costs in the general population results from individuals with low- and intermediate-level symptom patterns. As a result, small improvements among these individuals can result in greater overall improvements in the public health than larger improvements among those with the most severe symptoms."[5]

The National Gambling Impact and Behavior Study found 2.5 million pathological gamblers, 3 million problem gamblers, and 15 million at-risk gamblers in the United States. The same study found that the lifetime economic costs associated with problem gamblers were about half of the costs associated with pathological gamblers.[6] If the lifetime economic costs associated with at-risk gamblers are half the costs of problem gamblers, then the 15 million at-risk gamblers in the United States represent lifetime economic costs of $37.5 billion—a significantly greater sum than the approximately $26 billion in lifetime economic costs associated with pathological gamblers, and nearly equal to the $40 billion in lifetime economic costs for problem and pathological gambling together. As with other disorders, even small improvements among individuals at the less severe end of the problem gambling continuum are likely to result in significant overall improvements in the public health, as well as reductions in the economic costs of problem gambling. Furthermore, since individuals with less severe problems, whether with alcohol, drugs, or gambling, are more likely to be responsive to social attitudes and policy interventions, the emphasis on public awareness and education about problem gambling by key organizations in the field seems appropriate.

Treatment for Problem Gambling

The first help available for problem gamblers in the United States was Gamblers Anonymous. Gamblers Anonymous was established in California in the 1950s and has grown from only a few chapters in the early 1960s to thousands of chapters all over the United States as well as throughout the world at the end of the 1990s.[7] Gamblers Anonymous resembles other twelve-step programs in that it has no formal membership process or dues requirements; the only requirement for membership is a desire to stop gambling. Longtime members of Gamblers Anonymous serve as sponsors to newcomers, and anonymity is emphasized. Other similarities are that Gamblers Anonymous is not allied with any sect, denomination, political organization, or institution; does not accept outside donations; and does not engage in lobbying.

Gam-Anon, a fellowship for friends and families of gamblers, was chartered as a nonprofit organization in 1960 and is now headquartered in New York City. Although there are fewer Gam-Anon than Gamblers Anonymous meetings, there are still hundreds worldwide. A friend or family member can attend Gam-Anon even if the problem gambler is not attending Gamblers Anonymous. Like Gamblers Anonymous, membership in Gam-Anon is voluntary and open to anyone affected by gambling problems. There are no fees for membership, anonymity is a tradition, and Gam-Anon does not accept outside donations or grants.

In 1972, the Veterans Administration (VA) established the first professional treatment programs for pathological gamblers. Between 1972 and 1985, several more such programs were established at Veterans Administration Medical Centers around the country. By 1992, however, partly as a consequence of general cutbacks in funding for veterans' medical care, most of the VA's gambling treatment programs had been closed down. All of these programs, located within Veterans Administration Medical Center alcohol treatment units, consisted of inpatient treatment modeled on approaches developed for use in treating alcoholism.

In the 1980s and 1990s, a growing number of state governments began funding treatment services for problem gamblers. In 1985, only four states (Connecticut, Maryland, New Jersey, and New York) funded such services for problem gamblers. More recently, a think tank on state-funded treatment programs for problem gamblers, convened by the Massachusetts Council on Compulsive Gambling, included representatives from programs in thirteen states.[8] Figure 5.1 includes information on the availability of state-funded treatment in the different states.

In addition to state-funded treatment programs, there are now several private, for-profit hospitals that offer inpatient treatment services for problem gamblers. However, the number of beds available to problem gamblers in hospital settings is very small compared to the number of beds available to patients receiving treatment for alcohol or substance abuse. Furthermore, there is no uniformity in the standards of care or in the certification of inpatient programs that provide treatment to problem gamblers.

Professional treatment programs are generally staffed by licensed mental health or addictions treatment professionals, including psychiatrists, clinical psychologists, and social workers. Nearly all of these programs offer a "multi-modal" approach that includes educational and therapeutic interventions, individual and group therapy, psychiatric assessments, legal interventions, training in stress reduction, relapse prevention, coping skills and problem solving, and financial planning.[9]

In 1998, the first treatment program for problem gamblers providing a full continuum of care opened in Indianapolis.[10] Trimeridian is an unusual private and public sector hybrid, started by a small group of venture capitalists who believe that there will eventually be a substantial market for problem gambling treatment services. Trimeridian's program includes diagnosis and assessment, inpatient and outpatient treatment programs, an array of family programs, and aftercare. The company has several locations, including the inpatient Custer Center located in Indianapolis and outpatient treatment centers in Indianapolis and Las Vegas. The staff includes psychologists, certified gambling counselors, addiction counselors, psychiatrists, and family therapists.[11]

While the professional and self-help approaches are distinct, there are close ties between Gamblers Anonymous and professional treatment programs. Gamblers Anonymous represents a significant source of referrals to professional treatment programs, and many programs require or strongly advocate attendance at Gamblers Anonymous as part of their therapeutic regime. Like Gamblers Anonymous, most of the professional treatment programs in the United States have established abstinence from gambling and restitution of gambling-related debts as primary treatment goals. Internationally, researchers and treatment professionals are far more willing to consider alternative measures of treatment success, including reductions in debt, improved relationships with family and friends, and heightened self-esteem.[12]

No state government has yet required treatment professionals to obtain a separate license to provide counseling to problem gamblers and their families. Some states do encourage counselors to become certified as gambling counselors. Certification is available at the national level through certification boards of the National Council on Problem Gambling, the Massachusetts-based American Academy of Health Care Providers in the Addictive Disorders, and the New Jersey–based American Compulsive Gambling Counselor Certification Board. State-level certification is also available in several jurisdictions. Certification standards vary in eligibility requirements, hours required specifically in problem gambling training, hours required in clinical supervision, and testing requirements.

Outside of specialized programs, mental health and substance abuse treatment professionals rarely screen their clients for gambling involvement or gambling problems. Even when a gambling problem or pathology is identified, these professionals are often uncertain about the appropriate referrals to make or treatments to recommend. While there is a growing range of treatment options available for problem gamblers—including hospital inpatient programs for individuals who are seriously depressed or suicidal, outpatient programs in mental health and/or addiction settings that offer individual and group counseling, and self-help groups—there remains a need for professional training to give nonspecialists the tools they need to identify and refer, or even treat, individuals with gambling problems among their own clientele. There is also a need for training for other social service providers working in agencies where problem gamblers or their families may seek help—credit counseling agencies, bankruptcy courts, domestic violence shelters, child abuse agencies, law enforcement agencies, and the courts.

How Effective Are Gambling Treatment Programs?

There are only a few outcome studies of the effectiveness of treatment for gambling problems. The research that has been done suggests that multi-modal approaches to treating problem gambling are "effective in gamblers achieving and maintaining abstinence at least over the course of six months to one year."[13] In the United States, abstinence from gambling remains *the* criterion for success common across the different approaches and programs that are now available. According to this criterion, Gamblers Anonymous has a success rate of approximately 9 percent, while professional treatment programs, both inpatient and outpatient, have success rates that hover around 55 percent.

In truth, very little is known about the effectiveness of any of the treatment programs available to problem gamblers. This is partly due to the fact that most of these programs have not been in operation long enough for performance reviews and outcome studies to be completed. Another complication is that measures to assess and evaluate these programs are not well developed. While some states, such as Minnesota and Oregon, have started the evaluation process, it will be some time before this information becomes generally available.

In the 1980s, researchers at the Veterans Administration Hospital at Brecksville, Ohio, published outcome data for inpatient treatment for pathological gamblers.[14] In a twelve-month follow-up of 125 clients enrolled in this program, 48 percent responded to a mail survey. Over half of these clients (55 percent) had been abstinent for the entire year, and an additional 27 percent had been abstinent for at least one month. In a later, six-month follow-up of sixty-six clients from the same program, 86 percent were interviewed by telephone. Two-thirds of these clients (67 percent) reported periods of abstinence, and the researchers also detected significant improvements in subjective distress, impulse control, role impairment, alcohol abuse, and suicidal ideation.

Another early study examined the effectiveness of outpatient treatment for problem gambling.[15] Data comparing eighty-eight clients at intake and termination showed significant reductions in gambling involvement and improvements in social relations and lifestyle by the time treatment was completed. In a separate assessment of the same outpatient treatment program, comparison of ninety clients at intake and termination showed decreases in indebtedness as well as reductions in the frequency of gambling, preoccupation with gambling, and quarrels with family members, friends, and employers.[16]

More recently, outcome data were published for six outpatient treatment programs for problem gamblers in Minnesota. Treatment completion rates varied considerably among the programs, from a high of 87 percent to a low of 29 percent. A uniform evaluation of these programs found that 77 percent of clients reported no gambling at discharge, and 55 percent reported no gambling both at six months and one year after treatment. Improvement was also reported in areas of psychosocial functioning, frequency of gambling, indebtedness, and financial problems.[17]

Another recent evaluation of problem gambling outpatient treatment comes from Oregon.[18] Data from an evaluation of the twenty-six outpatient treatment programs there showed that only 20 percent of clients enrolled in these programs between 1995 and 1998 completed treatment. At six months, 42 percent of those completing treatment were contacted; nearly two-thirds of these individuals (64 percent) had not gambled in the past six months. At one year, 63 percent of these clients had not gambled in the past six months.

The published success rates for problem gambling treatment programs must be treated with caution. Problem gamblers entering treatment are not at all representative of the full spectrum of individuals experiencing problems related to their gambling.[19] Their motivation for achieving and sustaining abstinence is much higher than for less seriously compromised gamblers. Published reports of treatment effectiveness are biased further by extremely high dropout rates, common across all treatment modalities. Additionally, there is little information about recidivism among clients in these programs. While clients who complete treatment show substantial rates of success, it is likely that a significant proportion of the clients who drop out of treatment return one or more times to attempt treatment again, thereby adding to the overall costs of problem gambling to society. Finally, it must be noted that abstinence is only one of many possible measures of treatment effectiveness. Improvements in psychological functioning, interpersonal relationships, and quality of life are all important measures that could be assessed to determine the overall effectiveness of different treatment modalities. Until adequate funding and efforts are dedicated to the evaluation of treatment for problem gamblers, the question of what form or forms of treatment are most effective will remain unanswered.

Results from a recent longitudinal study of problem gamblers in New Zealand raise several additional considerations related to problem gambling service design and deployment.[20] In the New Zealand study, only about a quarter of the individuals identified as probable pathological gamblers in 1991 remained "pathological" in 1998, and only about one-third of those identified as problem gamblers remained in that category. Not one of these individuals reported in 1998 that they had sought help for their gambling problems. There were strong indications that problem gamblers were much more likely than probable pathological gamblers to become "nonproblematic" over time, suggesting that problem gamblers may be a more transient group than probable pathological gamblers. The New Zealand researchers found that preferences for horse race betting, and higher scores on problem gambling screens in 1991 were significantly related to 1998 problem gambling outcomes. Problem and pathological gamblers with co-morbid alcohol problems in 1991 were also less likely to show improvement in 1998.

These findings have potentially important implications for the design of problem gambling prevention and treatment programs. For example, in both the alcoholism and gambling fields there have been debates about the degree to which people can return to "controlled" or nonproblematic drinking or gambling. In the alcohol field, controlled drinking appears to be a more likely outcome for younger drinkers with less severe problems. The New Zealand longitudinal data suggest that while some patterns of nonproblematic gambling can be sustained, other patterns of gambling participation may increase the risk of relapse into problematic gambling. While the sample in the New Zealand longitudinal study was small, these data present several intriguing hypotheses that warrant further investigation.

RESEARCH ON PROBLEM GAMBLING

Historically, gambling in America has been regulated by the states. As lotteries, and then casinos, were legalized in numerous states in the 1980s and 1990s, debates arose about the impacts of widespread gambling legalization. While gambling proponents emphasized the economic benefits that could be produced (for example, jobs, investment, economic development, and tax revenues), gambling opponents stressed the likely social costs, including problem gambling, crime, and impacts on youths. While media and public attention focused on the "visceral, emotional" drama of the contest between proponents and opponents,[21] state governments responded by establishing services for problem gamblers. The immediate need created by these programs for information about the number and characteristics of problem gamblers in the community fostered the rapid growth of problem gambling prevalence research throughout the 1990s. Table 5.1 presents information about the earliest state-level problem gambling prevalence surveys conducted in the United States.

A review of the problem gambling research literature in 1985 showed that only two statewide surveys of gambling participation and problem gambling prevalence had been carried out—in Ohio and in the Delaware Valley, which encompasses Atlantic City and the Philadelphia metropolitan area.[22] In 1986, the first prevalence survey using the South Oaks Gambling Screen was carried out in New York State.[23] This survey served as a pilot for a proposal, funded by the National Institute of Mental Health in 1988, to carry out similar surveys in five more states, all but one of which had recently established publicly funded services for problem gamblers.[24]

During the 1990s, a growing number of states funded prevalence surveys to determine the number of problem and pathological gamblers in their jurisdiction and their characteristics. Figure 5.2 (page 78)

TABLE 5.1. EARLY PREVALENCE SURVEYS
IN THE UNITED STATES

	YEAR	SAMPLE SIZE	PROBLEM GAMBLING SCREEN	PATHOLOGICAL GAMBLING PREVALENCE RATE (%)	PUBLISHED ARTICLE
Delaware Valley	1984	534	CCSM	3.4	Sommers, 1988
Ohio	1985	801	CCSM	2.5	Culleton, 1985
New York	1986	1000	SOGS	1.4	Volberg & Steadman, 1988
New Jersey	1988	1000	SOGS	1.4	Volberg & Steadman, 1989
Maryland	1988	750	SOGS	1.5	Volberg & Steadman, 1989
Massachusetts	1989	750	SOGS	2.3	Volberg, 1994
Iowa	1989	750	SOGS	0.1	Volberg, 1994
California	1990	1250	SOGS	1.2	Volberg, 1994

Sources: Ira Sommers, "Pathological Gambling: Estimating Prevalence and Group Characteristics," *International Journal of the Addictions* 23 (1988): 477–90; Robert P. Culleton, *A Survey of Pathological Gamblers in the State of Ohio* (Philadelphia: Transition Planning Associates, 1985); Rachel A. Volberg and Henry J. Steadman, "Refining Prevalence Estimates of Pathological Gambling," *American Journal of Psychiatry* 145 (1988): 502–505; Rachel A. Volberg and Henry J. Steadman, "Prevalence Estimates of Pathological Gambling in New Jersey and Maryland," *American Journal of Psychiatry* 146 (1989): 1618–19; Rachel A. Volberg, "The Prevalence and Demographics of Pathological Gamblers: Implications for Public Health," *American Journal of Public Health* 84, no. 2 (1994): 237–41.

presents information about states where prevalence surveys have been conducted since 1986, when the South Oaks Gambling Screen was first used in New York State.

Prevalence research remained a major focus of investigation in the field of gambling studies for nearly a decade. However, in the wake of the passage of the National Gambling Impact Study Commission Act of 1996, the American Gaming Association established the National Center for Responsible Gaming (NCRG) to fund peer-reviewed research on problem and underage gambling.[25] NCRG is a nonprofit organization, governed by a board of directors evenly split between representatives of the casino industry and other sectors of the economy. NCRG follows a process similar to that established by the National Institutes of Health for reviewing grants from academic researchers.

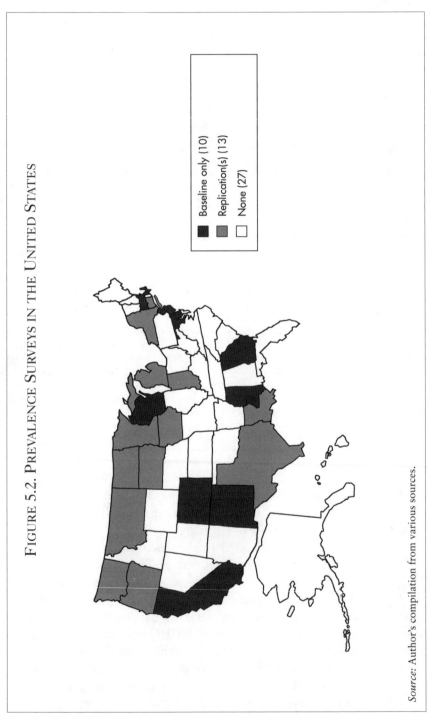

FIGURE 5.2. PREVALENCE SURVEYS IN THE UNITED STATES

Baseline only (10)
Replication(s) (13)
None (27)

Source: Author's compilation from various sources.

Between 1996 and 1999, NCRG was the largest source of funding for research on problem gambling in the United States. Since 1996, this organization has committed approximately $3 million to fund about twenty research projects in the areas of epidemiology, neuroscience, and social and behavioral sciences. The bulk of this funding (42 percent) has gone to Harvard University's Division on Addictions, headed by Howard Shaffer. The Harvard Project on Gambling and Health is committed to producing meta-analyses of problem gambling prevalence surveys, to conducting surveys of casino employees, and to producing and distributing the *WAGER*, a weekly newsletter on gambling-related research and news. Another 31 percent of the funding from NCRG has gone to research projects focused on the genetics and neuroscience of problem gambling. The remaining 27 percent has gone to projects on youth gambling, cognitive research, and identifying effective treatments for problem gambling.[26] Recently, NCRG announced that the academic and scientific functions of the center would be handed over to a new Harvard-based organization, the Institute for Research on Pathological Gambling and Related Disorders.[27]

In 1997, the National Gambling Impact Study Commission was charged with conducting a comprehensive study of the social and economic impacts of gambling in the United States, including an assessment of problem gambling. Although the commission spent more than half of its $4 million budget on new research initiatives, the commissioners unanimously concluded in their final report that one of the defining characteristics of the field was the "dearth of impartial, objective research that the public and policymakers at federal, tribal, state, and corporate levels need to shape public policies on the impacts of legal gambling."[28]

One response to this dearth of research was initiated in 1998 by the National Institutes of Health. A "special emphasis" panel was established to solicit problem gambling research proposals for a period of three years. This action did not mean that any special funds were set aside for problem gambling research; any proposals reviewed by this panel would still compete with the thousands of other proposals reviewed by the National Institutes of Health every year. However, this step did ensure that researchers without a background in gambling studies but with pilot data or interesting questions would be encouraged to undertake the arduous process of developing proposals for submission.

While more than twenty proposals were received for the first round of reviews for this special emphasis panel, the second round was much smaller. Nevertheless, by fiscal year 2000, the National Institutes of Health had awarded nine grants in the area of problem gambling, representing a commitment of approximately $9 million. These projects include a national survey of the co-occurrence of problem gambling and other disorders; the addition of gambling modules to two existing longitudinal studies; investigations of biological factors associated with problem gambling and evaluation of several different treatments for problem gamblers; development of an intervention to help spouses of problem gamblers; and a genetic study of gambling problems among male, middle-aged twins.[29]

FUNDING FOR PROBLEM GAMBLING SERVICES

In 1985, only four states funded any services for problem gamblers. In 1998, there were services of some kind for problem gamblers in twenty-one states. Altogether, these programs received approximately $22 million in funding from a range of sources, including state governments, gaming companies, and foundations. This level of funding represents only 0.1 percent of the $18 billion in gaming taxes collected by state governments in 1998 and an even smaller proportion of the gross revenues flowing annually to legal gambling industries in the United States.[30] The funds were spent on a range of services, including public education and outreach, prevention, training, treatment, and research.

Legislation permitting the expansion of gambling has created opportunities for advocates for problem gamblers to obtain funding for specialized programs. Such opportunities most often arise when state lotteries are permitted to expand their product line to include linked systems of video keno and video poker machines. In Nebraska, for example, Big Red Keno provided initial funding for the Nebraska Council on Compulsive Gambling. In New York, 3 percent of revenues from Quick Draw, the state lottery's five-minute keno game, is set aside for problem gambling programs. Similarly, in Oregon, legislation permitting the lottery to operate video poker required that 3 percent of the game's revenues be distributed for problem gambling services. Other opportunities arise when pari-mutuel facilities are permitted to expand to include gaming machines. Funding for problem gambling services in Delaware, for example, grew when slot machines were added at Delaware racetracks.

In 1998, the National Council on Problem Gambling conducted a review of funding for problem gambling services in the United States at the request of the National Gambling Impact Study Commission. While the results of the survey showed that $22 million were spent on problem gambling services in the United States in 1998, no funds at all were spent in thirteen of the forty-seven states with legal gambling. In states where problem gambling services are funded, the average amount spent per capita was $0.20. The survey also showed that spending on problem gambling services was highly concentrated, with the top four states that fund such services (Delaware, Iowa, Oregon, and Minnesota) accounting for 41 percent of the total spending on problem gambling services in the entire United States.

To place these data in context, it is instructive to compare funding for problem gambling services in the United States with funding for such services in other countries. A recent study in Canada found that expenditures on problem gambling programs totaled about $10 million, or $0.45 per person (in United States currency).[31] In the Australian states and territories, spending on problem gambling services is approximately $14 million, or $0.99 per person (in United States currency).[32] To fund problem gambling services in the United States at the level that these services are funded in Canada, it would be necessary to spend approximately $87 million. To fund problem gambling services at the level they are funded in Australia, it would be necessary to spend approximately $195 million. While this would represent a ninefold increase in current spending on problem gambling services, it would still represent only 1 percent of the $18 billion in tax revenues from legal gambling that flow to state governments annually.

Like funding, delivery of problem gambling services varies by state. The most common approach is for a state agency, most often overseeing substance abuse or mental health services, to make grants to or manage contracts with one of the affiliates of the National Council on Problem Gambling. Another approach is for the state agency to provide services directly through its existing service delivery network. Research may be conducted by a state agency, by a state university, by a collaborative effort between the two, or by a contract with an independent research firm. Some states have provided funding specifically for prevalence surveys on problem gambling. Other states have included prevalence surveys as part of larger impact studies of legal gambling.

PROBLEM GAMBLING AS AN INTELLECTUAL
AND ACADEMIC ISSUE

Since the 1980s, institutions of higher education have become increasingly active in the field of problem gambling. For example, the University of Nevada, Reno, houses the Institute for the Study of Gambling and Commercial Gaming. While activities at the institute are not confined to the issue of problem gambling, it is a cosponsor, with the National Council on Problem Gambling, of the *Journal of Gambling Studies*. Elsewhere in the state, the library at the University of Nevada, Las Vegas, houses the Gaming Research Center, one of the largest collections of books and materials related to gambling in the world. The Gaming Research Center serves as a resource for researchers and scholars interested in the history, psychology, sociology, and economics of gambling. In the United States as a whole, a growing number of institutions are developing gambling courses within their schools of management and business administration. Some of these programs include efforts to address the issue of problem gambling.

An important event in raising awareness about problem gambling among academic researchers was the establishment of the National Research Council's Committee on the Social and Economic Impact of Pathological Gambling. This committee was convened at the request of the National Gambling Impact Study Commission, and its report was published in 1999.[33] The committee included thirteen members, only four of whom were familiar with gambling issues generally and only three of whom had any background in problem gambling research or treatment. The exposure of the nongambling specialists on this committee to the issues of problem gambling has laid the foundation for a substantial increase in the number of researchers interested in investigating problem gambling. Several colleges and universities now offer courses for training counselors in the field of problem gambling. Other institutions are fostering research, either through their undergraduate schools, medical schools, or other graduate-level programs. The participation of college students in gambling activities also has led some colleges and universities to expand their on-campus counseling services to include problem gambling or to hold seminars to acquaint athletic directors with issues of problem gambling.

There also has been growth in the number of academic opportunities, nationally and internationally, to exchange ideas and information about problem gambling. Since 1979, the Institute for the Study of Gambling and Commercial Gaming has hosted the International Conference on Gambling and Risk Taking every three years. The proceedings of these conferences have included many important academic papers on problem gambling. The National Council on Problem Gambling holds an annual conference, and many of the National Council's state affiliates hold annual statewide or regional conferences where researchers and treatment professionals can exchange information about how to recognize and treat problem gamblers and their families.

Internationally, there has been growing attention to the issue of problem gambling in Australia, Canada, and Europe. In Australia, the National Association for Gambling Studies—a group of researchers, industry executives, and treatment professionals—holds an annual conference largely devoted to problem gambling research, awareness, and treatment issues, as does the European Association for the Study of Gambling. Several provinces in Canada, including Alberta and Ontario, have hosted conferences on problem gambling. Recent annual conferences of the World Health Organization's International Institute on the Prevention and Treatment of Dependencies have included entire tracks on problem gambling.

The gambling industries, too, are paying increasing attention to problem gambling in their annual trade conferences and expositions. Seminars on problem gambling have been included in both regional and national conferences on Indian gaming. Both the annual conferences of the North American Association of State and Provincial Lotteries and the Gaming Exposition and Congress, attended by representatives of all the gaming industries as well as by gaming regulators and product vendors, have included sessions on problem gambling for several years.

Interest in problem gambling also is growing among professional and trade associations. In addition to the American Psychiatric Association's recognition of pathological gambling in its *Diagnostic and Statistical Manual,* the American Medical Association and the New England Medical Association both have adopted resolutions on problem gambling to encourage physicians to advise their patients of the risks of gambling and to encourage state governments to fund education, prevention, and treatment programs.

6

THE POLICY CHALLENGES

The recent growth in legal gambling in America has taken place largely in the absence of any deliberative process within the states, on tribal lands, or by the federal government. Instead, policies have grown through a process of incremental and disconnected decisions, with rivalry and competition for revenues as common factors.[1]

While state and tribal governments, as well as the federal government, have benefited from the operation and regulation of gambling activities, they have done little to protect citizens from the negative effects of the activities from which these benefits are derived. Public confusion and uncertainty about the impacts of legal gambling on society does not excuse policymakers and other stakeholders from the need to address the full range of benefits and costs associated with legal gambling in America. Problem gambling should be a component in any cost-benefit analysis of gambling activities. It also should be a consideration in planning for and regulating all forms of legal gambling.

Economists have debated the extent of positive and negative consequences of the expansion of legal gambling in America. On the positive side of the ledger, proponents point to the billions of dollars in gambling privilege taxes that flow to state and tribal governments, as well as increased jobs and capital investment.[2] Although often neglected, another positive effect of legal gambling is the difficult-to-quantify value of the recreation that consumers derive from gambling: the fun that ordinary people have playing bingo or blackjack or betting on the ponies.[3] Commentators have argued that gambling provides important health benefits, such as a sense of connectedness, a change of pace, and a respite from social isolation or the demands of everyday life.[4] There is some evidence that certain patterns of gambling involvement may contribute to personal well-being and self-esteem.[5]

On the other side of the ledger, there are a variety of negative impacts associated with the availability of legal, commercial gambling. While critics cite crime and underage gambling, the Achilles' heel of legal gambling remains problem gambling.[6] As discussed in previous chapters, problem gambling affects a significant proportion of the American population and results in a long list of individual and social dysfunctions.

Formulating rational public policy is never easy. Decisions must be based on the expected outcomes of given actions and on accurate assessments of the benefits and costs of those actions. As the National Gambling Impact Study Commission has pointed out, the rapid expansion of legalized gambling, the very recent rise of gambling as a subject of study, and the dearth of reliable information on the benefits or costs of legal gambling have posed particular challenges to the development of gambling public policy.[7] I would add several additional concerns:

- the polarization of debates about gambling legalization and its impacts;

- the rapidly evolving nature of gambling activities;

- the existence of inadequate and outdated laws for regulating gambling; and

- the lack of planning and coordination among state and tribal governments and federal agencies with regard to legal gambling.

The Polarized Debate over Social Issues

I noted in Chapter 3 that a backlash to the rapid expansion of legal gambling in the United States has emerged since the mid-1990s. Some groups of Americans, particularly fundamentalist Christians, believe that gambling is sinful, and the current heavy consumer spending on legal gambling is a source of discomfort to them. Other Americans are persuaded that the costs of the operation of commercial gambling exceed the benefits.[8] Individuals and organizations holding these views are working diligently to oppose the expansion of legal gambling and to prevent new types of gambling from becoming legal.

The commercial gambling industries, like the alcohol and tobacco industries, are linked to an externality that is both peculiar to their customers and highly controversial. The gambling industries believe that the choice they have is between two business models: the early engagement of beer, wine, and liquor manufacturers and distributors in "responsible drinking" programs, on the one hand, and the long-standing resistance to the imposition of consumer-protection measures by the tobacco industry, on the other.

LESSONS FROM ALCOHOL

In the nineteenth century, the Temperance Reform movement polarized the country over the issue of alcohol. In the aftermath of World War I, the Eighteenth Amendment to the Constitution and the enforcing Volstead Act were passed, criminalizing both the consumption and distribution of alcoholic beverages. While it may have been a moral triumph, Prohibition was a catastrophe as public policy. Supporters of the Volstead Act believed that curtailing the supply of alcoholic beverages both was enforceable and would reduce demand and, thereby, consumption. Despite vigorous enforcement, Prohibition failed to accomplish any of these goals. Instead of falling, consumption of alcoholic beverages actually *increased*. The rising demand for alcohol, with its implied profitability, attracted suppliers undeterred by the fact that distilling and distributing liquor was a federal crime. However unintended the result, Prohibition forcibly transferred ownership of the liquor industry from licensed, legitimate companies to organized crime. Consumer protections were eliminated in the process. Dangerous and even lethal alcoholic beverages moved through the illicit distribution system; alcohol blindness and death were direct consequences.[9]

Repeal of the Volstead Act in 1933 coincided with the emergence of a new view of the ills associated with alcohol. In the wake of the formation of Alcoholics Anonymous in the 1930s and the development of the field of alcohol studies, growing numbers of Americans came to accept the view of alcoholism as a disease. Professional treatment for alcoholism, including early drug therapies, started to become available. In the 1950s and 1960s, prominent professional associations, including the American Medical Association, the American Public Health Association, and the American Psychiatric Association, took official notice of alcoholism, identifying it as a treatable disorder and calling for a broad expansion of treatment services. The 1970s saw even greater efforts to recognize and address alcohol problems. Congress established the National Institute on Alcohol Abuse and Alcoholism in 1970 to coordinate federal and state efforts to research and treat alcoholism. Diagnostic criteria for alcohol and drug dependence were established, and insurance companies began to include alcoholism treatment as a standard part of health care coverage.

During the 1980s, the focus of advocates shifted from treatment to prevention. Grassroots organizations, concerned about continuing high rates of alcohol consumption, particularly among youths, began working to change behaviors connected to alcohol consumption. Public figures spoke out about their own experiences with alcohol abuse and recognition grew of the effects of alcohol on women. The federal government mandated a national minimum drinking age and tied this to the availability of federal funding for highways. Public service advertising about the dangers of alcohol burgeoned and, again mandated by federal law, warning labels began to appear on all alcoholic beverage containers.[10]

The new view of alcoholism as a disease did not escape the attention of the companies producing liquor, beer, and wine. Beginning in the 1980s, America's distillers and, later, vintners began organizing in an effort to demonstrate their corporate commitment to social responsibility. Their argument is similar to the argument made more recently by the gambling industries: the vast majority of people who enjoy alcoholic beverages do so responsibly, there is work to be done to prevent the irresponsible use of alcoholic beverages, and the alcoholic beverage industry is prepared to shoulder some of the burden by engaging in public education and prevention. The major American distillers have spent more than $100 million to address the carefully chosen issues of drunk driving and underage drinking. These companies have worked to build local coalitions with law enforcement agencies, college and university administrators, and alcohol distributors.[11] As a result of this strategy, America's distillers have maintained a voice in national, state, and local debates about alcohol and have managed to guide legislation and regulation in directions favorable to their interests.

LESSONS FROM BIG TOBACCO

Although both alcohol and tobacco were targets of the Temperance Reform movement of the nineteenth century, efforts to limit the manufacture, sale, and consumption of tobacco products did not succeed until the 1990s. Like alcohol, tobacco use in America was widespread, especially after World War I. In contrast to alcohol, tobacco cultivation was an important agricultural crop and tobacco products were manufactured and sold by large, well-known companies. During World War II, tobacco became a part of the war effort: cigarettes were included in soldiers' C-rations and tobacco consumption soared. By 1949, between 44 and 47 percent of American adults smoked: over half of all men and one-third of all women.

Starting in the 1960s, a chorus of scientific, public health, and government opposition arose, probably led by the 1964 release of the first Surgeon General's report on the health hazards of smoking. Numerous laws and regulations aimed at limiting the availability and visibility of tobacco products were passed at the state and federal levels. Scientists and medical practitioners pointed increasingly to research demonstrating the health hazards associated with direct and "passive" exposure to tobacco products. Although the tobacco companies countered with research findings of their own, federal legislation was passed in 1969 requiring health warnings on cigarette packs. A year later, further legislation banned cigarette advertising on radio and television. Another blow came in the early 1980s, when life insurance companies began offering discounts for nonsmokers based on actuarial research showing significant differences in mortality between smokers and nonsmokers. The 1980s also saw the beginning of a wave of restrictions on smoking in public, first in the workplace, then on airline flights, and eventually in restaurants, bars, airports, office buildings, and public places of all kinds. One measure of the effectiveness of the campaign against smoking is found in statistics on tobacco use. Surveys show that between 1965 and 1990, adult smoking in the United States declined from 42 percent to 25 percent.

The major tobacco companies responded by diversifying into other, more consumer-friendly product lines, such as beer and frozen foods. In selling tobacco products, these companies increasingly focused on overseas markets, particularly the developing countries of Asia and Africa, where restrictions on advertising and distribution were less onerous. While continuing publicly to deny research evidence that cigarette smoking was harmful, the tobacco industry made enormous campaign donations to national, state, and local politicians and sought to prevent any federal rulings that tobacco was a drug or that smoking constituted a significant public health hazard.

The efforts of the tobacco companies to stave off litigation and industry regulation were unsuccessful. Starting in the early 1990s, a growing number of state attorneys general initiated suits against the major tobacco companies to recover medical costs associated with smoking among the indigent. (This group eventually included attorneys general from forty-six states and five territories.) A 1997 settlement exchanged Federal Drug Administration regulation of nicotine as a drug, money for antismoking campaigns, and bans on vending machines and outdoor advertising for restrictions on tobacco makers' liability.[12]

WHAT CAN BE LEARNED?

There are informative parallels and differences in the social histories of alcohol, tobacco, and gambling. For example, while the physical and psychological health problems associated with alcohol and gambling were not initially defined in this way, both were eventually and successfully "medicalized." In contrast, the issues associated with tobacco use have been defined as health problems since the 1950s, in spite of vigorous resistance from tobacco companies and other stakeholders.

Clearly, public attitudes about the consumption of alcohol and tobacco have been challenged and changed over the second half of the twentieth century. Public attitudes toward gambling also have changed, although widespread views about appropriate levels of consumption of gambling have yet to emerge. Critical elements affecting changing attitudes toward alcohol and tobacco have been the involvement of the insurance industry and the federal government in shaping coverage for health problems associated with the use of these substances, in shaping the media messages related to consumption and prevention, and in sponsoring research on the etiology of alcohol and tobacco addiction as well as the effectiveness of prevention and treatment efforts.

The lessons from alcohol and tobacco suggest that criminalization of widely accepted behaviors may not work as well as efforts to influence social norms through public debate and policy. With regard to gambling, the challenge is to bring all of the stakeholders—gambling operators, lawmakers, regulators, treatment professionals, researchers, and gamblers and their families—to the table and to ensure that their concerns are heard and reflected in the legislative and regulatory responses of the many levels of government involved.

A MOVING TARGET

An important feature of legal gambling at the end of the twentieth century is constant innovation. Gambling operators, whether private or public entities, are entrepreneurs in highly competitive markets.[13] Competition has led indirectly to a blurring of the boundaries between what were once considered "soft" and "hard" forms of gambling and to the merging of gambling with other, previously unassociated activities.

In the 1980s, the differences between "soft" forms of gambling (that is, lotteries and bingo) and "hard" forms of gambling (that is, casino-style games and pari-mutuel wagering) were clear. This boundary blurred as lotteries started to offer a multitude of games besides the traditional, large-jackpot drawings—daily numbers games, then instant or scratch tickets, and, finally, electronic gaming devices offering keno, poker, blackjack, and line games such as those offered on slot machines at casinos. A similar process occurred in the horse racing industry, as off-track betting and simulcasting spread in the 1980s and, then, as racetracks added slot machine and card club operations to their traditional product in the 1990s.

The 1990s saw major expansions in casino-style gambling outside the former monopoly markets of Nevada and Atlantic City. Casino-style gambling outside these markets came first to the small mining towns of Colorado and South Dakota, where limited-stakes table games, such as poker and blackjack, along with slot machines were legalized. Like many lotteries, the tax revenues generated by these operations were initially set aside for historical preservation. These provisions were soon discarded and the tax revenues channeled directly into the states' general funds.

Following passage of the Indian Gaming Regulatory Act of 1988 and the success of limited-stakes casinos in Colorado and South

Dakota, several states up and down the Mississippi Valley legalized riverboat casino gambling. Strict limits on both wagers and losses were placed on the first riverboats, legalized in Iowa in 1991. Within a few years, riverboat casinos had been legalized and had become operational in Illinois, Missouri, Indiana, Louisiana, and Mississippi. While riverboat casinos in most of these states must be located on facilities that look like boats, few actually leave shore. As the industry developed, the betting and loss limits as well as the cruising requirement in Iowa were lifted in 1994 so that its operations would remain competitive with those in nearby markets. Up and down the Mississippi River, the term "dockside gambling" is now a more accurate description of these casinos than "riverboat gambling."

The monopoly held by Nevada and, later, Atlantic City on casino-style gambling was further eroded, first by the spread of casino-style games to racetracks and off-track betting facilities, then by the growth of tribal gaming operations in many states, and finally by the expansion of gaming machines into venues that did not previously offer any type of gambling. To compete with the growing availability of local casino-style gambling, casinos in the major markets of Nevada, New Jersey, and Mississippi now market themselves as "family entertainment" and offer a range of activities to visitors, including theme parks, shopping, dining, and shows.

THE REGULATION OF GAMBLING

Law and jurisprudence have a tendency to lag behind society, and the laws related to gambling are no exception. The U.S. Congress has enacted a variety of laws pertaining to gambling over the course of the twentieth century, most of which have dealt with the issue from the perspective of interstate commerce. For example, laws were passed by Congress in the early part of the century that prohibited any advertising of lotteries and the transportation of gambling devices across state lines. However, most gambling operations come under the purview of the states rather than Congress. Even in Nevada, operation of a gambling enterprise is viewed as a "privilege," quite different from running a restaurant, a factory, or a farm. As a result,

> the shape and operation of legalized gambling has been largely a product of [state and tribal] government decisions. . . .

> Governments determine which kinds of gambling will be permitted and which will not; the number, location, and size of establishments allowed; the conditions under which they operate; who may utilize them and under what conditions; who may work for them; even who may own them. . . . And, because [state, local, and tribal] governments determine the level and type of competition to be permitted . . . they also are a key determinant of the various industries' potential profits and losses.[14]

While state and tribal governments have had much to say about how gambling operations will be organized and run, they have had little to say, until very recently, about what gambling operators must do to protect their customers from the risks of problem gambling. A number of state governments, including Massachusetts, New York, and Oregon, have mandated that a small percentage of revenues from new gambling operations, usually "convenience gambling" of one kind or another, be set aside for problem gambling services. In Missouri, when riverboat gambling was introduced, casinos were required to operate self-exclusion programs for customers concerned about their gambling. In 1999, the Nevada Gaming Commission published its first regulations requiring Nevada casinos to post problem gambling helpline numbers and brochures prominently around their properties and to provide gaming employees with training about problem gambling.

As Nelson Rose has noted, "the lawmakers of the land have much less incentive than the [gambling] entrepreneurs to keep their eyes open to the many ways ingenious individuals have of getting around the intent of the law."[15] One difficulty is that few lawmakers understand the complexities of the gambling industries sufficiently to be able to predict the likely effects of specific legislation on gambling operators and consumers. Inconsistent interpretation of existing legislation is also common; for example, the refusal of the Federal Communications Commission to classify tournaments as a form of gambling led to rapid growth in slot machine tournaments at casinos in the 1980s and 1990s.[16] Finally, there are numerous instances where lawmakers inadvertently legalized one or another type of gambling. Examples include:

- The brief establishment of "accidental casinos" in Pennsylvania in the mid-1980s when the liquor code was amended to allow dart and billiard tournaments without obtaining a permit—addition of a single word to the liquor code amendment opened the door to card game tournaments that quickly became popular among Atlantic City casino dealers, who were not permitted to gamble in any Atlantic City casinos.

- The explosion of video poker in South Carolina in the mid-1990s after the state legislature determined that the game constituted a "lottery" rather than "gambling."

- The Indian Gaming Regulatory Act of 1988 (IGRA), passed at a time when the federal government was cutting back on financial assistance to Native Americans living on reservations. Most of the lawmakers who supported IGRA thought that they were voting to permit Native Americans to operate bingo games; few understood that the law would open the door to casino gambling in every state where federally recognized Indian tribes held land.

- The Professional and Amateur Sports Protection Act, passed in 1992, which prohibited betting on sports events throughout the nation (with a few grandfathered exceptions), technically making criminals of everyone who puts money into an office Super Bowl pool.

WHAT CAN THE STATES AND TRIBES DO?

The alternative to the prohibition of legal gambling in America is effective regulation and adequate monitoring. For regulation to be effective, state and tribal governments, as well as the federal government, must engage in a conscious and deliberative process toward this end. There is a need to update laws regulating all types of gambling in America and to establish a regulatory and enforcement framework that will be effective in the present as well as in the future. A key element will be assigning responsibility for the regulation of legal gambling to a single agency, at each level of government, charged with balancing the positive and negative impacts of all kinds of gambling within a jurisdiction. Finally, since regulation cannot work effectively without good information, there is a need for extensive monitoring of the impacts of legal gambling on individuals and communities and for dissemination of this information to stakeholders.

Few state governments have established a single agency with responsibility for regulating all types of gambling. More commonly, regulation and enforcement of charitable gambling, lotteries, pari-mutuel wagering, and casino gambling are overseen by separate agencies. In many cases, these agencies reflect the competitive pressures among the industries they regulate and there is little effort at coordination or cooperation. In fact, it is more common for these agencies to grant regulatory concessions to operators that they oversee in an effort to maintain a "level playing field," as was discussed in Chapter 3. To complicate matters further, issues of problem gambling rarely are addressed by gambling regulatory agencies. Instead, when they are funded, problem gambling prevention and treatment services are channeled through government agencies with responsibilities for health and social welfare. Little consideration is given by the agencies responsible for regulating gambling to the social impacts of these activities.

There is a need to improve communication and coordination between gambling regulatory bodies and the health and human service agencies that must respond to the needs of problem gamblers and their families. While the many affiliates of the National Council on Problem Gambling frequently fill this role informally, it will be important to formalize and increase such communication and coordination in the future.

All of the major gambling markets are regional—for example, Nevada appeals to California citizens, New Jersey markets to New York, and Louisiana markets to Texas. As a result, the governments that regulate and benefit from gambling in these markets are not the governments that must ultimately cope with the impacts of problems arising from these activities. Consequently, there is a need for coordination among the states and tribes with regard to the provision of services for problem gamblers and their families.

The North American Gaming Regulators' Association regularly brings representatives together from many states and provinces to address issues of gambling regulation and enforcement. The National Council on Problem Gambling performs a similar function on the problem gambling side. Better communication between the constituencies represented by these groups is needed, as well as better coordination of efforts by regulatory and social service agencies in different jurisdictions.

WHAT CAN THE FEDERAL GOVERNMENT DO?

The federal situation is similar to that of the state governments. The National Gambling Impact Study Commission identified gambling on Indian lands, Internet gambling, and gambling on military installations as issues of federal concern and left responsibility for all other types of gambling in the hands of the states. While this division of labor seems sensible, the federal government has yet to acknowledge its responsibilities to regulate even these three types of gambling and to monitor their impacts.

Indian gaming regulation is overseen by a newly constituted federal agency, the National Indian Gaming Commission. The National Indian Gaming Commission is a small and underfunded agency with responsibility for regulating hundreds of tribal gaming operations. The Bureau of Indian Affairs, within the Department of the Interior, and the Indian Health Service, within the Department of Health and Human Services, have no clear responsibility for the regulation of Indian gambling or for examining the impact of legal gambling on reservations.

The situation with regard to military gambling is similar: the Department of Defense has done little to address the question of the impacts of gambling on its personnel or even on military readiness. While the Department of Defense maintains thousands of slot machines on overseas bases, the relationship between these machines and gambling problems among military personnel has never been examined.[17] While a few questions about gambling problems were included in surveys of alcohol and drug abuse among active-duty personnel in 1992 and 1998,[18] there is only one treatment program for problem gamblers on active duty and no department-wide policies with regard to problem gambling.[19]

In response to congressional pressure, the Department of Health and Human Services has given some attention to the issue of problem gambling. A special program announcement from the National Institutes of Health, first published in 1998, and efforts to add gambling modules to a number of major health-related surveys conducted by the department have resulted in what will be a substantial increase in funding for gambling research over the next five years. The Substance Abuse and Mental Health Services Administration has moved more slowly to address the issue of problem gambling. In September 2000, the Center for Mental Health Services contracted with the National Council on Problem Gambling to develop a white paper on problem gambling prevention, treatment, and measures to track gambling behavior and conducted a symposium on problem and pathological gambling within the context of mental health services. However, there has been little effort to coordinate the burgeoning research and treatment initiatives within the federal government with any efforts by regulatory or enforcement agencies, such as the Departments of Commerce and Justice.

Gambling on the Internet remains a controversial issue. The initial congressional response to Internet gambling has been an effort to criminalize it through legislation such as the Internet Gambling Prohibition Act.[20] It may already be too late: both Nevada and New Jersey are considering bills to legalize Internet gambling in their states.[21] Once the states legalize Internet gambling, it is difficult to predict how federal lawmakers will respond. If Internet gambling does become legal throughout the United States, it will be necessary to establish a regulatory framework to oversee the operators and to institute funding mechanisms to address the negative impacts that the widespread availability of gambling within the home can be expected to produce.

Although not without difficulties, gambling on the Internet probably can be regulated. In fact, if governments would take a proactive approach to this issue, it may be possible to create the world's most tightly regulated gambling market. The fact that Internet gambling is conducted in a networked, data-intensive environment offers opportunities for regulation and oversight in several critical areas, including licensure, testing for game integrity and site security, auditing and oversight, taxation, and consumer protection.

With regard to problem gambling, the Internet has potential for oversight that surpasses even the most highly regulated "brick and mortar" casinos. Within the data-intensive environment of the Internet, every detail of every gambling transaction can be recorded and, potentially, analyzed. Players "chasing losses" or exhibiting other behaviors that are indicative of problem gambling could be flagged and their betting habits further analyzed. Internet gambling sites could be required to have information about problem gambling present on players' screens at all times. Licensed gambling sites could be required to have links to help lines and problem gambling counselors. Furthermore, players could have the ability to set their own predetermined betting limits and to exclude themselves from play. All of these measures could be monitored to assess their effectiveness in minimizing gambling-related problems on the Internet.

A final federal consideration is the need to consider stricter regulation of activities that begin to look like gambling, such as day trading. While little research has been done on this topic to date, some day traders engage in behaviors—such as "chasing"—that are hallmarks of problem gambling. Eventually it will be desirable to bring all of the gambling regulatory efforts at the federal level together within a single agency. However, this probably lies several decades in the future.

THE NEED FOR PLANNING AND COORDINATION

While gambling on Indian lands, Internet gambling, and gambling on military installations are concerns that the federal government may be willing to address, many of the oversight functions left to the states and tribes are unlikely to be filled. This is at least partly due to the awkward position in which state and tribal governments find themselves, as both the regulators and operators of legal gambling activities.[22] One consequence of the blurring of the boundaries between governments as regulators and providers of gambling has been a failure on the part of state and tribal governments—and the federal government—to monitor gambling and problem gambling in a coherent and systematic fashion.

There is much to be done to keep track of the impacts of gambling and problem gambling in America in the coming decades. The federal government can, and must, play a role in overseeing the monitoring of gambling behavior and problem gambling prevalence and in assisting states and tribes to refine their problem gambling services. Such efforts are needed to enable states and tribes to respond effectively to the public health threats posed by their involvement in legal, commercial gambling.

In spite of the rapid expansion of legal gambling, few steps have been taken by policymakers to manage the growth of legal gambling in a responsible manner. If the goal of government is to maximize the net benefits of legal gambling, then several critical steps are necessary. These include striking a balance between permitting gambling activities and protecting the gambling public, as well as ongoing monitoring and assessment of the impacts of gambling on individuals, families, and communities.[23]

ASSISTING THE STATES AND TRIBES

I noted in Chapter 4 that the number of states conducting prevalence surveys of gambling and problem gambling increased rapidly in the 1990s, as the availability of legal gambling expanded and as constituents, and then policymakers, became concerned about the negative impacts of these activities. Clearly, the states have been at the forefront of efforts to identify patterns of gambling involvement in the general population as well as changes in problem gambling prevalence over time. However, interpreting the results of these surveys can be difficult because of variations in the time period between baseline and replication surveys as well as in the quality of these projects from one state to the next. To date, no state government has plans in place to conduct such surveys on an ongoing basis. Furthermore, few of these state surveys include samples large enough to examine changes in gambling participation and problem gambling prevalence among subgroups in the population.

In considering the best approach to monitoring changes in gambling and problem gambling over time, I believe that some questions are best answered using state-level data while other questions are better answered on the basis of information generated at the federal level. I endorse the recommendation of the National Gambling Impact Study Commission that states conduct prevalence surveys on a regular basis, although perhaps not as frequently as every two years as the commission suggests.[24] Such surveys would provide detailed information about changes in gambling participation and problem gambling prevalence over time. States differ greatly in the characteristics of their populations as well as in the features of different gambling activities available to their citizens, so state-level prevalence surveys are an essential tool to monitor the impacts of gambling and problem gambling within the states. In some cases, it might be feasible for states to organize cooperatively to conduct prevalence surveys for a region of the country. In other instances, states and tribes could cooperate in conducting prevalence surveys. The recent replication survey in North Dakota, funded jointly by the state government and the tribes, is an example of the value of this approach.

Some sort of clearinghouse is also needed to gather information from state-level studies of gambling behavior and impacts, to synthesize this information, and to provide states, tribes, and the federal government with information about the impacts of gambling in different regions of the country and in relation to different types of gambling. A clearinghouse also could be a critical source of information on the best practices in conducting gambling impact studies. Other areas where a clearinghouse could serve in the policymaking process would be in conducting regular surveys of problem gambling services and in evaluating the effectiveness of the numerous state-level and national problem gambling help lines that currently operate with little or no government oversight. The National Council on Problem Gambling has attempted to fulfill some of these functions in recent years, although, without reliable sources of funding and support, these efforts largely have been in response to needs expressed by the council's state affiliates or to requests from the federal government.

FEDERAL INITIATIVES

There are other questions about gambling and its impacts that cannot be answered at the state level. This is largely due to the enormous cost of some research initiatives and to the need for multiyear commitments of funding. Some of these questions relate to the etiology of problem and pathological gambling—how people get involved with gambling, how they get into trouble with gambling, and how some of them get out of trouble. I have noted that the need for longitudinal research on gambling careers is particularly acute. Other questions are comparative in nature—how do the impacts of widespread electronic gambling devices in Montana compare with the impacts of tribal casinos in North Dakota? How does the introduction of a state lottery in South Carolina affect state lotteries in contiguous states?

I envision a two-pronged approach to implementing federal studies of gambling and problem gambling. The first effort would involve adding modules to assess gambling involvement and problem gambling to longitudinal studies that are already under way, as has already happened with the National Survey of Health and Life Experiences of Women. Although not a longitudinal survey, the addition of a gambling module to the replication National Comorbidity Survey will yield much-needed information about the co-morbidity of problem and pathological gambling with other mental disorders. Another possibility is to add a short gambling module to the National Household Survey on Drug Abuse, an extremely large survey conducted annually by the Substance Abuse and Mental Health Services Administration. Addition of a gambling module to a longitudinal survey of youths, such as the Monitoring the Future study, would dramatically improve our understanding of the impacts of the availability of legal gambling on teenagers and children.

The second effort would involve the federal government conducting regular surveys at the national level of gambling involvement, gambling expenditures, and problem gambling prevalence. Conducting a national survey every five years would provide the federal government with critical information about changes in the availability of legal gambling and would permit comparisons across regions of the United States. The federal government has only conducted two national prevalence surveys, twenty-five years apart, both carried out under contract to federally mandated commissions. To ensure the success of this effort, it would be necessary to identify the most appropriate federal agency or agencies to conduct such surveys—perhaps as a joint venture by the Department of Commerce and the Department of Health and Human Services—and to establish an advisory group of gambling researchers and other scientists to oversee the effort and ensure both the comparability of results between studies and the incorporation of new measures and designs as these become available.

The federal government is also in a better position than the individual states to establish and maintain a database on the impacts of gambling, including participation and expenditures as well as health, family, workplace, financial, and legal impacts. As with the clearinghouse recommended above, this could be accomplished through contracts with academic institutions or not-for-profit agencies, although care would be needed to ensure that this database remained relevant to the needs of state and tribal agencies and the federal government. It would be advisable for the agency or organization responsible for maintaining this database also to have responsibilities for disseminating information about gambling and problem gambling to the many stakeholders concerned with these issues, including legislators, regulators, gambling operators, researchers, treatment professionals, gamblers, and their families.

A MODEL FOR THE FUTURE

A growing number of national governments in Asia and Europe have begun to establish *gambling monitoring systems* that assess the impacts of legal gambling on citizens and communities over extended periods of time. Gambling monitoring systems serve both policy analysis and research needs. A good monitoring system includes the capacity for follow-up and evaluation studies as well as for generating early warning of changes in the impacts of existing and new gambling activities. Such systems are based on the establishment and maintenance of an integrated database, the development and refinement of monitoring tools, and additional basic research into specific topics. When fully developed, such systems offer policymakers, the gambling industries, and health and human service agencies a neutral database for strategic analysis and decision making to promote responsible gambling and to implement services that meet the needs of problem gamblers and their families.

A model gambling monitoring system must include two basic elements. The first is an *integrated database* that includes information about gambling participation, gambling problems, and gambling expenditures as well as other, related sources of data, such as help-line calls and availability of services. It is essential that the integrated database be kept up-to-date, theoretically and methodologically, both to reflect changing conceptions of gambling and gambling problems and to incorporate new research data from other studies. The second element is a *basic research effort* that could include a variety of projects generating information to inform both policy analysis and service development. Several basic research needs in the gambling field, including longitudinal research on groups of people over time to improve our understanding of how gambling problems develop, studies of help seeking by problem gamblers, and studies of the effectiveness of problem gambling services, are particularly critical. There are also needs for studies of the impacts of specific gaming introductions on communities and studies of gambling among school-age children. As noted above, one critical element to any such system is to establish a process for dissemination so that responses to new developments or information can be made quickly.

THE EXAMPLE OF NEW ZEALAND

The case of New Zealand is a useful illustration of what can be done to address the issues of gambling and problem gambling in a comprehensive manner. When legal gambling in New Zealand began to expand in the mid-1980s, the New Zealand government centralized oversight of all legal gambling in the Department of Internal

Affairs. As in other jurisdictions, the gaming industries in New Zealand initially resisted the argument that problem gambling was a unique negative externality. However, under pressure from the Department of Internal Affairs and other concerned stakeholders, the major gaming industry groups in New Zealand were persuaded to join the Committee on Problem Gambling Management (COPGM) and to contribute to the ongoing funding of problem gambling services and research. COPGM includes representatives from all of the legal gambling operations in New Zealand as well as treatment providers and representatives of key community groups. Each sector of the industry is required to make financial contributions to support problem gambling services, based on a negotiated formula that includes gross revenues, number of outlets, and level of advertising, among other factors.

Initially, funding from COPGM provided for a national gambling help line run by the Compulsive Gambling Society of New Zealand, as well as support for some specialist counseling services provided by existing nonprofit alcohol and drug treatment agencies. The Department of Internal Affairs has used revenues from legal gambling operations in New Zealand to conduct gambling participation surveys every five years and to track consumer spending on all types of legal gambling. In addition, two comprehensive surveys of gambling and problem gambling have been funded through the Department of Internal Affairs, the latter with some assistance from COPGM.

The structure of problem gambling services in New Zealand is unique in that these services are predominantly funded by the gambling industries and remain, to some extent, independent of public mental health and alcohol and drug services. However, the structure developed in New Zealand for monitoring the impacts of legal gambling over time and for coordinating oversight of these activities has reduced the prevalence of problem gambling in New Zealand and increased the ability of New Zealanders to find help for their gambling problems.[25]

CLOSER TO HOME: THE EXAMPLE OF OREGON

The introduction of video poker by the Oregon Lottery in 1992 included a measure stating that 3 percent of gross revenues from these games would be spent on services for problem gamblers. After several legal challenges, the legislature changed this approach; the funds for these services are now allocated from general revenues. Oregon currently spends approximately $2 million per year for problem gambling services.

When this funding stream was first established in Oregon, the revenues were distributed to county mental health agencies through the Association of Oregon County Mental Health Programs (AOCMHP). The association, and later the Oregon Gambling Addiction Treatment Foundation, which was spun out of AOCMHP, contracts for independent data collection and program evaluation services for all of the county programs and provides training in problem gambling detection and treatment for mental health and alcohol and drug abuse treatment professionals throughout the state. In addition, the foundation has contracted for several prevalence surveys in Oregon, including baseline and replication studies in the adult population as well as surveys of adolescents and seniors. The board of the foundation includes representatives of the Oregon Lottery and tribal casinos in the state, as well as community leaders and stakeholders such as the Oregon Restaurant Foundation.

There are now twenty-six programs in Oregon that receive funding for problem gambling services, including education and outreach, treatment services, and a twenty-four-hour help line that handles several thousand calls each year. All of the problem gambling services in Oregon are overseen by the Office of Alcohol and Drug Abuse, with advice from a Problem Gambling Services Advisory Committee. The gambling program manager in the Office of Alcohol and Drug Abuse works closely with the gambling regulatory commissions in Oregon and sits on the board of the Oregon Gambling Addiction Treatment Foundation.

The development of problem gambling services in Oregon was not entirely smooth. Nevertheless, this example serves to underscore the importance of several key elements in the successful implementation of problem gambling services—the need for a reliable source of funding, the need to bring a range of stakeholders together to plan and coordinate, and the need to implement a broad array of services, including education, prevention, outreach, treatment, evaluation, and research. The benefits of reliable funding and rational planning in Oregon are perhaps best seen in the significant decrease in the prevalence of problem gambling in Oregon detected between 1997 and 2000.[26]

WHERE DO WE GO FROM HERE?

If nothing else, our tour of the issues surrounding legal gambling and problem gambling in America has illustrated the lack of initiative that has evolved from the failure to develop a unified institutional base to promote rational policymaking and conduct objective research with regard to legal gambling. An important reason for conducting problem gambling research is to assess both the positive and adverse impacts of various forms of gambling in a particular community or society. In the field of gambling studies, prevalence surveys often have been the first, and sometimes the only, tool adopted by governments to assess the impacts of gambling in a jurisdiction. However, prevalence surveys are only one of many sources of information that should be considered in undertaking comprehensive social impact assessments, or cost-benefit analyses, of gambling in society. Problem gambling research will be of more value to policymakers and stakeholders if studies incorporate a range of sources of information, including surveys, clinical data, and attitudinal studies, as well as a broad conceptual framework that examines the effects that legal gambling can have throughout economic and social systems. Such studies will be more likely to contribute to the advancement of scientific understanding of gambling and problem gambling if they are closely linked to relevant bodies of knowledge and address hypotheses that arise from them.[27]

I noted in 1994 that "in spite of recent increases in public awareness of pathological gambling as a treatable disorder and the increased availability of treatment services for individuals with gambling-related problems, [the proliferation of legalized gambling in the United States] has yet to be conceptualized in meaningful public health terms."[28] David Korn and Howard Shaffer recently echoed this call for the adoption of a public health perspective to understanding and responding to gambling and problem gambling in America and internationally.[29] In contrast to the narrower, clinical concerns framed by the "medical" model of problem gambling, a public health perspective offers a broad view: one that does not focus solely on questions of gambling addiction, but on a balance of costs and benefits. A public health perspective provides policymakers and health practitioners with a range of strategies to minimize the negative impacts and maximize the potential benefits of legal gambling, strategies that can incorporate multiple levels of prevention, treatment, and rehabilitation as well as actions by a multitude of stakeholders.

For this perspective to succeed, however, policymakers, public health professionals, gaming industry representatives, researchers, treatment professionals, and others will have to actively frame the issue in these terms. All of these stakeholders will have to work together to shape the evolution of gambling and problem gambling in American society and to develop innovative approaches for helping individuals who experience problems when they gamble. It is incumbent on all of us to work together to prevent gambling problems from occurring and to ensure that services are available to those whose lives are disrupted by gambling.

NOTES

CHAPTER 2

1. Max W. Abbott and Rachel A. Volberg, *Gambling and Problem Gambling in the Community: An International Overview and Critique* (Wellington: New Zealand Department of Internal Affairs, 1999), p. 77.

2. This narrative is a composite from the stories of several Gamblers Anonymous members interviewed for Clive Gammon, "Tales of Self-Destruction," *Sports Illustrated,* March 10, 1986, pp. 64–72.

3. Rachel A. Volberg and Henry J. Steadman, "Accurately Depicting Pathological Gamblers: Policy and Treatment Implications," *Journal of Gambling Studies* 8, no. 4 (1992): 402.

4. John DiConsiglio, "She Gambled with Her Life," *Redbook,* February 2000, pp. 112–16.

5. Henry R. Lesieur, "Costs and Treatment of Pathological Gambling," *Annals of the American Academy of Political and Social Science* 556 (1998): 154–55. See also Sue Cox et al., *Problem and Pathological Gambling in America: The National Picture* (Columbia, Md.: National Council on Problem Gambling, 1997), pp. 8–10.

6. Howard J. Shaffer, Matthew N. Hall, and Joni Vander Bilt, "Estimating the Prevalence of Disordered Gambling Behavior in the United States and Canada: A Research Synthesis," *American Journal of Public Health* 89, no. 9 (1999): 1373. See also Brian Castellani, *Pathological Gambling: The Making of a Medical Problem* (Albany: State University of New York Press, 2000), pp. 197–98.

7. American Psychiatric Association, *Diagnostic and Statistical Manual of Mental Disorders,* 3d ed. (Washington, D.C.: American Psychiatric Association, 1980), reprinted in National Research Council, *Pathological*

Gambling: A Critical Review (Washington, D.C.: National Academy Press, 1999), pp. 273–75.

8. American Psychiatric Association, *Diagnostic and Statistical Manual of Mental Disorders,* 4th ed. (Washington, D.C.: American Psychiatric Association, 1994), reprinted in National Research Council, *Pathological Gambling,* pp. 278–82.

9. Henry R. Lesieur and Richard J. Rosenthal, "Pathological Gambling: A Review of the Literature, Prepared for the American Psychiatric Association Task Force on DSM-IV Committee on Disorders of Impulse Control Not Elsewhere Classified," *Journal of Gambling Studies* 7, no. 1 (1991): 7–8.

10. Max W. Abbott, Maynard Williams, and Rachel A. Volberg, *Seven Years On: A Follow-up Study of Frequent and Problem Gamblers Living in the Community* (Wellington: New Zealand Department of Internal Affairs, 1999), pp. 89–93.

11. See Linda Berman and M. E. Seigel, *Behind the Eight-Ball: A Guide for Families of Gamblers* (New York: Simon & Schuster, 1992); Mary Heineman, *Losing Your Shirt* (Center City, Minn.: Hazelden, 1992). Both cited in Loreen J. Rugle, *The Treatment of Pathological Gambling,* report prepared for the Indiana Gambling Impact Study Commission (Indianapolis: Center for Urban Policy and the Environment, Indiana University, 1999).

12. Herb Kutchins and Stuart A. Kirk, *Making Us Crazy—DSM: The Psychiatric Bible and the Creation of Mental Disorders* (New York: Free Press, 1997); I. Nelson Rose, *Gambling and the Law* (Hollywood: Gambling Times, 1986).

13. Castellani, *Pathological Gambling,* pp. 19–40.

14. Peter Conley et al., *Harm Reduction: Concepts and Practice: A Policy Discussion Paper* (Ottawa: Canadian Centre on Substance Abuse, 1996), Section D-1, available at http://www.ccsa.ca/wgharm.htm.

15. Eric Single, "Harm Reduction as the Basis for Drug Policy: What Does It Mean and How Does It Matter?" paper presented at the Addictions Millennium 2000 Conference, Toronto, November 17, 2000, p. 26.

16. Productivity Commission, *Australia's Gambling Industries,* report no. 10 (Canberra, Australia: AusInfo, 1999), Chapters 11–21, available at http://www.indcom.gov.au/inquiry/gambling/finalreport.

17. Jackie Ferris, Harold Wynne, and Eric Single, *Measuring Problem Gambling in Canada: Final Report, Phase I of the Inter-Provincial Task Force on Problem Gambling* (Toronto: Canadian Centre on Substance Abuse, 1999), Chapter 4, available at http://www.ccsa.ca/Final1.htm.

18. National Research Council, *Pathological Gambling,* Chapter 5.

19. Abbott and Volberg, *Gambling and Problem Gambling in the Community,* Chapter 3. See also Volberg and Steadman, "Accurately Depicting Pathological Gamblers," pp. 401–20.

20. National Research Council, *Pathological Gambling,* Chapter 5. See also Cox et al., *Problem and Pathological Gambling in America,* pp. 14–17.

21. Lesieur, "Costs and Treatment of Pathological Gambling," pp. 155–57. See also Valerie C. Lorenz and Robert A. Yaffee, "Pathological Gambling: Psychosomatic, Emotional and Marital Difficulties as Reported by the Gambler," *Journal of Gambling Behavior* 2, no. 1 (1986): 40–49.

22. Robert L. Custer and Lillian F. Custer, "Characteristics of the Recovering Compulsive Gambler: A Survey of 150 Members of Gamblers Anonymous," paper presented at the Fourth National Conference on Gambling, Reno, Nev., June 1978. See also Rena Nora, "Profile Survey on Pathological Gambling," paper presented at the Sixth National Conference on Gambling and Risk Taking, Atlantic City, N.J., June 1984.

23. Robert A. McCormick et al., "Affective Disorders among Pathological Gamblers Seeking Treatment," *American Journal of Psychiatry* 141 (1984): 215–18. See also Robert D. Linden, Harrison G. Pope, and Jeffrey M. Jonas, "Pathological Gambling and Major Affective Disorder: Preliminary Findings," *Journal of Clinical Psychiatry* 47 (1986): 201–203.

24. Paul E. Polzin et al., "From Convenience Stores to Casinos: Gambling—Montana Style," *Montana Business Quarterly* 36, no. 4 (1998): 2–14; William N. Thompson, Ricardo Gazel, and Dan Rickman, "The Social Costs of Gambling in Wisconsin," *Wisconsin Policy Research Institute Report* 9, no. 6 (1996): 1–44; Max W. Abbott and Rachel A. Volberg, *Frequent Gamblers and Problem Gamblers in New Zealand: Report on Phase Two of the National Survey* (Wellington: New Zealand Department of Internal Affairs, 1992); Sheila M. Specker et al., "Psychopathology in Pathological Gamblers Seeking Treatment," *Journal of Gambling Studies* 12, no. 1 (1996): 67–81; Garry J. Smith, Rachel A. Volberg, and Harold J. Wynne, "Leisure Behavior on the Edge: Differences between Controlled and Uncontrolled Gambling Practices," *Society and Leisure* 17, no. 1 (1994): 233–48; Dean R. Gerstein et al., *Gambling Impact and Behavior Study: Report to the National Gambling Impact Study Commission* (Chicago: National Opinion Research Center, 1999).

25. Cox et al., *Problem and Pathological Gambling in America.*

26. National Research Council, *Pathological Gambling,* pp. 127–39. See also Barry Spunt et al., "Pathological Gamblers in Methadone Treatment: A Comparison between Men and Women," *Journal of Gambling Studies* 12, no. 4 (1996): 431–49.

27. Randy Stinchfield and Ken C. Winters, *Treatment Effectiveness of Six State-Supported Compulsive Gambling Treatment Programs in Minnesota, Fourth and Final Report,* report to the Minnesota Department of Human Services (Minneapolis: University of Minnesota Medical School, 1996).

28. D. N. Crockford and N. el-Guebaly, "Psychiatric Comorbidity in Pathological Gambling: A Critical Review," *Canadian Journal of Psychiatry* 43 (1998): 43–50.

29. Rachel A. Volberg, *Gambling and Problem Gambling in New York: A 10-Year Replication Survey, 1986 to 1996,* report to the New York Council on Problem Gambling (Albany, N.Y.: New York Council on Problem Gambling, 1996).

30. Abbott, Williams, and Volberg, *Seven Years On,* pp. 81–85; Smith, Volberg, and Wynne, "Leisure Behavior on the Edge," pp. 233–48.

31. Gerstein et al., *Gambling Impact and Behavior Study,* pp. 29–31. See also ibid., Chapter 3.

32. Valerie C. Lorenz, "Differences Found among Catholic, Protestant and Jewish Families of Pathological Gamblers," paper presented at the Fifth National Conference on Gambling and Risk Taking, Lake Tahoe, Nev., June 1981.

33. Valerie C. Lorenz and Robert A. Yaffee, "Pathological Gambling: Psychosomatic, Emotional and Marital Difficulties as Reported by the Spouse," *Journal of Gambling Behavior* 4, no. 1 (1988): 13–26.

34. National Research Council, *Pathological Gambling,* pp. 158–59. See also Lorenz and Yaffee, "Pathological Gambling: Psychosomatic, Emotional and Marital Difficulties as Reported by the Spouse," pp. 13–26.

35. R. C. Bland et al., "Epidemiology of Pathological Gambling in Edmonton," *Canadian Journal of Psychiatry* 38 (1993): 108–12.

36. Polzin et al., "From Convenience Stores to Casinos," pp. 2–14.

37. Rachel A. Volberg, *Gambling and Problem Gambling in North Dakota: A Replication Study, 1992 to 2000,* report to the North Dakota Office of the Governor (Bismarck, N.D.: Office of the Governor, 2001), pp. 26–27.

38. Lorenz, "Differences Found among Catholic, Protestant and Jewish Families of Pathological Gamblers."

39. Durand F. Jacobs, "Illegal and Undocumented: A Review of Teenage Gambling and the Plight of Children of Problem Gamblers in America," in Howard J. Shaffer et al., eds., *Compulsive Gambling: Theory, Research, and Practice* (Boston: Lexington Books, 1989), pp. 275–78.

40. Henry R. Lesieur and Robert Klein, "Pathological Gambling among High School Students," *Addictive Behaviors* 12 (1987): 129–35.

41. Thompson, Gazel, and Rickman, "The Social Costs of Gambling in Wisconsin," p. 17. These costs are based on information from problem gamblers who sought help from Gamblers Anonymous and are significantly higher than costs reported in the U.S. national survey, which are derived from a representative sample of adults residing in the United States.

42. J. Terrence Brunner et al., *Casino Gambling in Chicago: Better Government Association Staff White Paper,* report prepared for the Chicago Metro Ethics Coalition (Chicago: Better Government Association, 1992), pp. 21, 117–20.

43. National Research Council, *Pathological Gambling,* p. 161.

44. Henry R. Lesieur, *Report on Pathological Gambling in New Jersey,* New Jersey Governor's Advisory Commission on Gambling, April 1988, p.

38; Robert M. Politzer, James S. Morrow, and Sandra B. Leavey, "Report on the Cost-Benefit/Effectiveness of Treatment at the Johns Hopkins Center for Pathological Gambling," *Journal of Gambling Behavior* 1, no. 2 (1985): 131–42.

45. Stinchfield and Winters, *Treatment Effectiveness of Six State-Supported Compulsive Gambling Treatment Programs in Minnesota,* pp. 31, 40–41.

46. Lorenz and Yaffee, "Pathological Gambling: Psychosomatic, Emotional and Marital Difficulties as Reported by the Spouse," pp. 13–26.

47. Lesieur, "Costs and Treatment of Pathological Gambling," p. 155.

48. C. Ison, "Dead Broke," *Star Tribune,* December 5, 1995, cited in National Research Council, *Pathological Gambling,* p. 161.

49. Henry R. Lesieur and Robert Klein, "Prisoners, Gambling and Crime," paper presented at the Annual Meeting of the Academy of Criminal Justice Scientists, Las Vegas, March–April 1985. See also Valerie C. Lorenz, *An Overview of Pathological Gambling* (Baltimore: National Center for Pathological Gambling, 1990).

50. These data are from a survey of Gamblers Anonymous members (N = 55) in Montana, completed in 1998 as part of a larger study of the impacts of gambling in Montana (for published results, see Polzin et al., "From Convenience Stores to Casinos").

51. Lesieur and Klein, "Prisoners, Gambling and Crime."

52. Polzin et al., "From Convenience Stores to Casinos," p. 14.

53. Gerstein et al., *Gambling Impact and Behavior Study.*

54. An intercept survey involves face-to-face interviews with individuals entering or exiting a specific location.

55. Henrik Harwood, D. Fountain, and G. Livermore, "Economic Costs of Alcohol Abuse and Alcoholism," in M. Galanter, ed., *Recent Developments in Alcoholism,* vol. 14 (New York: Plenum Press, 1998), cited in Gerstein et al., *Gambling Impact and Behavior Study,* p. 53.

56. Gerstein et al., *Gambling Impact and Behavior Study,* p. 54.

57. Lesieur and Rosenthal, "Pathological Gambling: A Review of the Literature," 5–40; Peter L. Carlton and Paul Manowitz, "Physiological Factors as Determinants of Pathological Gambling," *Journal of Gambling Behavior* 3, no. 4 (1988): 274–85; Alex P. Blaszczynski, Simon W. Winter, and Neil McConaghy, "Plasma Endorphin Levels in Pathological Gambling," *Journal of Gambling Behavior* 2, no. 1 (1986): 3–14; Alex P. Blaszczynski, Neil McConaghy, and Anna Frankova, "Boredom Proneness in Pathological Gambling," *Psychological Reports* 67: 35–42.

58. Sheila B. Blume, "Compulsive Gambling and the Medical Model," *Journal of Gambling Behavior* 3, no. 4 (1987): 237–47; Richard J. Rosenthal, "Pathological Gambling," *Psychiatric Annals* 22, no. 2 (1992): 72–78.

59. Sigmund Freud, "Dostoyevsky and Parricide," in James Strachey, ed., *The Complete Works of Sigmund Freud,* vol. 21 (London: Hogarth Press,

1961), pp. 61–70; Edmund Bergler, *The Psychology of Gambling* (London: International Universities Press, 1954); Richard J. Rosenthal, "Pathological Gambling," pp. 72–78.

60. John R. Graham and Beverly H. Lowenfeld, "Personality Dimensions of the Pathological Gambler," *Journal of Gambling Behavior* 2, no. 1 (1986): 58–66; Richard A. McCormick et al., "Personality Profiles of Hospitalized Pathological Gamblers: The California Personality Inventory," *Journal of Clinical Psychology* 43, no. 5 (1987): 521–27.

61. Alex P. Blaszczynski and Neil McConaghy, "Criminal Offenses in Gamblers Anonymous and Hospital Treated Pathological Gamblers," *Journal of Gambling Studies* 10, no. 2 (1994): 99–127; Alex P. Blaszczynski and Neil McConaghy, "Antisocial Personality Disorder and Pathological Gambling," *Journal of Gambling Studies* 10, no. 2 (1994): 129–45; Graham and Lowenfeld, "Personality Dimensions of the Pathological Gambler," pp. 58–66; J. D. Moravec and P. H. Munley, "Psychological Test Findings on Pathological Gamblers in Treatment," *International Journal of the Addictions* 18 (1983): 1003–9; Lesieur and Rosenthal, "Pathological Gambling," pp. 5–40.

62. W. E. Glassman, "Female Pathological Gamblers: Early Trauma and Depression," Ph.D. diss., Professional School of Psychology, San Francisco, 1990.

63. Blase Gambino et al., "Perceived Family History of Problem Gambling and Scores on SOGS," *Journal of Gambling Studies* 9, no. 2 (1993): 169–84; Rina Gupta and Jeffrey L. Derevensky, "Familial and Social Influences on Juvenile Gambling Behavior," *Journal of Gambling Studies* 13, no. 3 (1997): 179–92.

64. Mark D. Griffiths, "The Role of Subjective Mood States in the Maintenance of Fruit Machine Gambling Behaviour," *Journal of Gambling Studies* 11, no. 2 (1995): 123–35; Durand F. Jacobs, "Evidence Supporting a General Theory of Addiction," in William R. Eadington and Juday A. Cornelius, eds., *Gambling Behavior and Problem Gambling* (Reno, Nev.: Institute for the Study of Gambling and Commercial Gaming, 1993), pp. 287–94.

65. K. P. Blum et al., "The D2 Dopamine Receptor Gene as a Determinant of Reward Deficiency Syndrome," *Journal of the Royal Society of Medicine* 89, no. 7 (1996): 396–400; David E. Comings et al., "A Study of the Dopamine D_2 Receptor Gene in Pathological Gambling," *Pharmacogenetics* 6 (1996): 223–34; Wendy Slutske et al., "Common Genetic Vulnerability for Pathological Gambling and Alcohol Dependence in Men," *Archives of General Psychiatry* 57 (2000): 666–73.

66. Alex P. Blaszczynski and Neil McConaghy, "The Medical Model of Pathological Gambling: Current Shortcomings," *Journal of Gambling Behavior* 5, no. 1 (1989): 42–52; R. Iain F. Brown, "Models of Gambling

and Gambling Addiction as Perceptual Filters," *Journal of Gambling Behavior* 3, no. 4 (1987): 224–36; John Rosecrance, "The Next Best Thing: A Study of Problem Gambling," *International Journal of the Addictions* 20 (1985): 1727–40.

67. D. B. Cornish, *Gambling: A Review of the Literature and Its Implications for Policy and Research* (London: Her Majesty's Stationery Office, 1978), cited in Robert W. Wildman, *Gambling: An Attempt at an Integration* (Edmonton, Canada: Wynne Resources, Inc., 1997); Mark G. Dickerson, *Compulsive Gamblers* (London: Longman, 1984); R. Iain F. Brown, "Classical and Operant Paradigms in the Management of Gambling Addictions," *Behavioral Psychotherapy* 15 (1987): 111–22.

68. Robert Ladouceur and Michael Walker, "A Cognitive Perspective on Gambling," in P. M. Salkovskis, ed., *Trends in Cognitive and Behavioural Therapies* (New York: John Wiley & Sons, 1996), pp. 89–120; L. Sharpe and N. Tarrier, "Towards a Cognitive-Behavioural Theory of Problem Gambling," *British Journal of Psychiatry* 162 (1993): 407–12.

69. Ladouceur and Walker, "A Cognitive Perspective on Gambling," pp. 89–120; Mark D. Griffiths, "The Cognitive Psychology of Gambling," *Journal of Gambling Studies* 6, no. 1 (1990): 31–42; Mark D. Griffiths, "The Role of Cognitive Bias and Skill in Fruit Machine Gambling," *British Journal of Psychology* 85 (1994): 351–69.

70. Basil R. Browne, "Going on Tilt: Frequent Poker Players and Control," *Journal of Gambling Behavior* 5, no. 1 (1989): 3–21; John Rosecrance, "Adapting to Failure: The Case of Horse Race Gamblers," *Journal of Gambling Behavior* 2, no. 2 (1987): 81–94.

71. Ladouceur and Walker, "A Cognitive Perspective on Gambling," pp. 89–120.

72. Robert Custer and Harry Milt, *When Luck Runs Out: Help for Compulsive Gamblers and Their Families* (New York: Facts on File, 1985), pp. 30–46; Henry R. Lesieur, *The Chase: Career of the Compulsive Gambler* (Cambridge, England: Schenkman, 1984), pp. 23–53.

73. Henry R. Lesieur and Sheila B. Blume, "When Lady Luck Loses: Women and Compulsive Gambling," in Nan van den Bergh, ed., *Feminist Perspectives on Addictions* (New York: Springer, 1991), pp. 181–97.

74. David Oldman, "Chance and Skill: A Study of Roulette," *Sociology* 8 (1974): 407–26; Thomas M. Holtgraves, "Gambling as Self-Presentation," *Journal of Gambling Behavior* 4, no. 2 (1988): 78–91; David M. Hayano, *Poker Faces: The Life and Work of Professional Card Players* (Berkeley: University of California Press, 1982); Thomas M. Martinez, *The Gambling Scene* (Springfield, Ill.: Charles C. Thomas, 1983); John Rosecrance, *The Degenerates of Lake Tahoe: A Study of Persistence in the Social World of Horse Race Gambling* (New York: Peter Lang, 1985); Leonard R. N. Ashley,

"'The Words of My Mouth, and the Meditation of My Heart': The Mindset of Gamblers Revealed in Their Language," *Journal of Gambling Studies* 6, no. 3 (1990): 241–61.

75. Alex P. Blaszczynski, "Pathways to Pathological Gambling: Identifying Typologies," *E-Gambling: The Electronic Journal of Gambling Issues* 1 (March 2000), available at http://www.camh.net/egambling; Abbott, Williams, and Volberg, *Seven Years On*, pp. 70–71, 89–91.

76. Castellani, *Pathological Gambling*; Howard J. Shaffer, Matthew N. Hall, and Joni Vander Bilt, *Estimating the Prevalence of Disordered Gambling Behavior in the United States and Canada: A Meta-analysis* (Boston: Harvard Medical School Division on Addictions, 1997); Ferris, Wynne, and Single, *Measuring Problem Gambling in Canada*.

77. National Research Council, *Pathological Gambling*, p. 140.

78. Linda Greenhouse, "Horse Sense," *New York Times*, November 6, 1998, p. B3; Hayano, *Poker Faces*; David McCumber, *Playing Off the Rail: A Pool Hustler's Journey* (New York: Random House, 1996).

79. John Rosecrance, "Playing the Horses Is Hard Work," *Sociology and Social Research* 71 (1986): 47–49.

80. Rachel A. Volberg et al., "Assessing Self-Reported Expenditures on Gambling," *Managerial and Decision Economics* (forthcoming).

CHAPTER 3

1. I. Nelson Rose, *Gambling and the Law* (Hollywood: Gambling Times, 1986); Herb Kutchins and Stuart A. Kirk, *Making Us Crazy—DSM: The Psychiatric Bible and the Creation of Mental Disorders* (New York: Free Press, 1997).

2. The Gallup Organization, "Gambling in America: Topline and Trends" (Princeton, N.J: Gallup Organization, 1999), available at http://www.gallup.com/poll/socialaudits/gambling2.asp.

3. C. Chapple and S. Nofziger, "Bingo!: Hints of Deviance in the Accounts of Sociability and Profit of Bingo Players," *Deviant Behavior* 21 (2000): 489–517; Rachael Dixey, "Bingo in Britain: An Analysis of Gender and Class," in Jan McMillen, ed., *Gambling Cultures: Studies in History and Interpretation* (London: Routledge, 1996); Joseph Hraba and Gang Lee, "Gender, Gambling and Problem Gambling," *Journal of Gambling Studies* 12, no. 1 (1996): 83–101; R. Evans, D. K. Gauthier, and C. J. Forsyth, "Dogfighting: Symbolic Expression and Validation of Masculinity," *Sex Roles* 39, no. 11/12 (1998): 825–38; Harry H. L. Kitano, *Japanese-Americans: The Evolution of a Subculture* (Englewood Cliffs, N.J.: Prentice-Hall, 1976); Stanford M. Lyman, *Chinese Americans* (New York: Random House, 1974); J. Henslin, "Craps and Magic," *American Journal of Sociology* 73 (1967): 316–30; Ivan Light,

"Numbers Gambling among Blacks: A Financial Institution," *American Sociological Review* 42 (1977): 892–904; Irving K. Zola, "Observations on Gambling in a Lower-Class Setting," in Howard S. Becker, ed., *The Other Side: Perspectives on Deviance* (New York: Free Press, 1964), pp. 247–60.

4. Rose, *Gambling and the Law*, pp. 1–2.

5. John M. Findlay, *People of Chance: Gambling in American Society from Jamestown to Las Vegas* (New York: Oxford University Press, 1986), pp. 44–78.

6. Rose, *Gambling and the Law*, pp. 1–2.

7. Commission on the Review of the National Policy Toward Gambling, *Gambling in America* (Washington, D.C.: U.S. Government Printing Office, 1976), Chapter 1.

8. National Gambling Impact Study Commission, *Final Report* (Washington, D.C.: U.S. Government Printing Office, 1999), Chapter 2, available at http://www.ngisc.gov.

9. Maureen Kallick et al., *Survey of American Gambling Attitudes and Behavior*, final report to the Commission on the Review of the National Policy Toward Gambling (Ann Arbor, Mich.: Survey Research Center, Institute for Social Research, 1976), Chapter 3; Eugene M. Christiansen, "The 1999 Gross Annual Wager of the United States," *International Gaming and Wagering Business* 21, no. 8 (2000): 15–17.

10. Eugene M. Christiansen, "An Overview of Gambling in the United States," testimony before the National Gambling Impact Study Commission, Virginia Beach, Va., February 8, 1999.

11. David Johnston, *Temples of Chance: How America Inc. Bought Out Murder Inc. to Win Control of the Casino Business* (New York: Doubleday, 1992), Chapter 2.

12. Vicki Abt, James F. Smith, and Eugene M. Christiansen, *The Business of Risk: Commercial Gambling in Mainstream America* (Lawrence: University Press of Kansas, 1985), pp. 234–47. See also William R. Eadington, "The Economics of Casino Gambling," *Journal of Economic Perspectives* 13, no. 3 (1999): 173–92.

13. Findlay, *People of Chance*, p. 157.

14. National Gambling Impact Study Commission, *Final Report*, p. 1-2.

15. I. Nelson Rose, "The Myth of the Level Playing Field," *Casino Executive* 49 (1999).

16. Ronald M. Pavalko, *Risky Business: America's Fascination with Gambling* (Belmont, Calif.: Wadsworth, 1999), p. 87.

17. Paul Doocey, "Gaming Scores in Michigan and Arizona," *International Gaming and Wagering Business* 17, no. 12 (1996): 1, 4; Viveca Novak, "They Call It Video Crack," *Time*, June 1, 1998, pp. 58–59.

18. Brian Castellani, *Pathological Gambling: The Making of a Medical Problem* (Albany: State University of New York Press, 2000), p. 126.

19. John Rosecrance, *Gambling without Guilt: The Legitimation of an American Pastime* (Belmont, Calif.: Wadsworth, 1988), pp. 3–6, 161–63.

20. Kallick et al., *Survey of American Gambling Attitudes and Behavior.*

21. Dean R. Gerstein et al., *Gambling Impact and Behavior Study: Report to the National Gambling Impact Study Commission* (Chicago: National Opinion Research Center, 1999).

22. Cited in The Gallup Organization, "Gambling in America."

23. Kallick et al., *Survey of American Gambling Attitudes and Behavior*, Table 1.1-1, p. 2; Gerstein et al., *Gambling Impact and Behavior Study*, Figure 1, p. 7.

24. Gerstein et al., *Gambling Impact and Behavior Study*, Figure 1a, p. 7.

25. Hraba and Lee, "Gender, Gambling and Problem Gambling"; Henry R. Lesieur and Sheila B. Blume, "When Lady Luck Loses: Women and Compulsive Gambling," in Nan van den Bergh, ed., *Feminist Perspectives on Addictions* (New York: Springer, 1991), pp. 181–97.

26. Kallick et al., *Survey of American Gambling Attitudes and Behavior,* Table 1.1-1, p. 2.

27. Hraba and Lee, "Gender, Gambling and Problem Gambling," Table 1, p. 92.

28. Rachel A. Volberg and Steven M. Banks, "A New Approach to Understanding Gambling and Problem Gambling in the General Population," paper presented at the Ninth International Conference on Gambling and Risk Taking, Las Vegas, June 1994.

29. Waiman P. Mok and Joseph Hraba, "Age and Gambling Behavior: A Declining and Shifting Pattern of Participation," in William R. Eadington and Judy A. Cornelius, eds., *Gambling Behavior and Problem Gambling* (Reno, Nev.: Institute for the Study of Gambling and Commercial Gaming, 1993), pp. 51–74.

30. The Gallup Organization, "Gambling in America."

31. Rachel A. Volberg, Marianna T. Toce, and Dean R. Gerstein, "From Back Room to Living Room: Changing Attitudes toward Gambling," *Public Perspective* 10, no. 5 (1999): 12.

32. Karl Heubusch, "Taking Chances on Casinos," *American Demographics*, May 1, 1997, available at http://www.demographics.com/publications.

33. Max W. Abbott and Rachel. A. Volberg, *Gambling and Problem Gambling in the Community: An International Overview and Critique* (Wellington: New Zealand Department of Internal Affairs, 1999), section 2.7, pp. 28–32; Sebastian Sinclair and Rachel A. Volberg, "Submission to the U.K. Gambling Review Body on Internet Gambling," U.K. Gambling Review Body, London, 2000.

34. National Gambling Impact Study Commission, *Final Report*, pp. 2-4–2-6, 3-11–3-12, 3-18, 7-30, Recommendation 7.4.

35. Rachel A. Volberg, *Changes in Gambling and Problem Gambling in Oregon, 1997 to 2000* (Salem: Oregon Gambling Addiction Treatment

Foundation, 2001); Rachel A. Volberg, *Gambling and Problem Gambling in North Dakota: A Replication Study, 1992 to 2000* (Bismarck, N.D.: Office of the Governor, 2001); Rachel A. Volberg and Walton L. Moore, "Gambling and Problem Gambling in Louisiana: A Replication Study, 1995 to 1998," Appendix D in Timothy P. Ryan and Janet F. Speyrer, *Gambling in Louisiana: A Benefit/Cost Analysis*, report to the Louisiana Gaming Control Board (New Orleans: University of New Orleans, 1999); Rachel A. Volberg and Walton L. Moore, *Gambling and Problem Gambling in Washington State: A Replication Study, 1992 to 1998*, report to the Washington State Lottery (Olympia: Washington State Lottery, 1999); Paul E. Polzin et al., "From Convenience Stores to Casinos: Gambling—Montana Style," *Montana Business Quarterly* 36, no. 4 (1998): 2–14.

36. For example, the rate of weekly gambling among respondents in Louisiana declined from 37 percent to 20 percent. This corresponds to a decline of 45 percent, calculated by dividing the difference between the two weekly gambling rates (–16.5 percent) by the 1995 baseline rate (36.9 percent).

37. Sebastian Sinclair, "U.S. May Be Missing the Mark on Internet Gaming," *International Gaming and Wagering Business* 21, no. 7 (2000): 12.

38. Volberg, *Changes in Gambling and Problem Gambling in Oregon*, pp. 11–13.

39. Social worlds consist of networks of people working cooperatively to produce the things that characterize that world. From this perspective, scientific theories or works of art are not the products of individuals but rather the joint products of all the people who cooperate via the characteristic conventions of the worlds of science or art to bring such "objects" into existence. Social worlds do not have sharp boundaries and they vary in the degree to which they are independent of interference with other organized groups in society. See Anselm Strauss, "A Social World Perspective," *Studies in Symbolic Interaction* 1 (1978): 119–28; Howard S. Becker, *Art Worlds* (Berkeley: University of California Press, 1982).

40. Kutchins and Kirk, *Making Us Crazy*.

41. Ibid.

42. Joseph A. Dunne, "Increasing Public Awareness of Pathological Gambling Behavior: A History of the National Council on Compulsive Gambling," *Journal of Gambling Behavior* 1, no. 1 (1985): 9.

43. Robert M. Lindner, "The Psychodynamics of Gambling," *Annals of the American Academy of Political and Social Science* 269 (1950): 93–107; Edmund Bergler, *The Psychology of Gambling* (London: International Universities Press, 1974).

44. Basil R. Browne, "The Selective Adaptation of the Alcoholics Anonymous Program by Gamblers Anonymous," in Eadington and Cornelius, *Gambling Behavior and Problem Gambling*, pp. 573–94.

45. Robert Custer and Harry Milt, *When Luck Runs Out: Help for Compulsive Gamblers and Their Families* (New York: Facts on File, 1985), pp. 294–307.

46. Dunne, "Increasing Public Awareness of Pathological Gambling Behavior."

47. Robert Goodman, *The Luck Business: The Devastating Consequences and Broken Promises of America's Gambling Explosion* (New York: Free Press, 1995), Chapter 8.

48. Castellani, *Pathological Gambling*, pp. 189–90.

CHAPTER 4

1. William Alonso and Paul Starr, eds., *The Politics of Numbers* (New York: Russell Sage Foundation, 1987); Elihu M. Gerson, "Scientific Work and Social Worlds," *Knowledge* 4 (1983): 357–79; Kenneth Prewitt, "Public Statistics and Democratic Politics," in Neil J. Smelser and Dean R. Gerstein, eds., *Behavioral and Social Science: Fifty Years of Discovery* (Washington, D.C.: National Academy Press, 1986), pp. 113–28; Albert J. Reiss, "Measuring Social Change," in Smelser and Gerstein, *Behavioral and Social Science*, pp. 36–72.

2. Theodore M. Porter, *Trust in Numbers: The Pursuit of Objectivity in Science and Public Life* (Princeton, N.J.: Princeton University Press, 1995), Chapters 6 and 7.

3. Henry R. Lesieur and Sheila B. Blume, "The South Oaks Gambling Screen (SOGS): A New Instrument for the Identification of Pathological Gamblers," *American Journal of Psychiatry* 144 (1987): 1184–88.

4. Rachel A. Volberg and Henry J. Steadman, "Refining Prevalence Estimates of Pathological Gambling," *American Journal of Psychiatry* 145 (1988): 502–5.

5. Howard J. Shaffer, Matthew N. Hall, and Joni Vander Bilt, *Estimating the Prevalence of Disordered Gambling Behavior in the United States and Canada: A Meta-analysis* (Boston: Harvard Medical School Division on Addictions, 1997); Max W. Abbott and Rachel A. Volberg, *Taking the Pulse on Gambling and Problem Gambling in New Zealand: Phase One of the 1999 National Prevalence Survey* (Wellington: New Zealand Department of Internal Affairs, 2000); Productivity Commission, *Australia's Gambling Industries*, report no. 10 (Canberra, Australia: AusInfo, 1999); Ibrahim Duvarci et al., "DSM-IV and the South Oaks Gambling Screen: Diagnosing and Assessing Pathological Gambling in Turkey," *Journal of Gambling Studies* 13, no. 3 (1997): 193–206; Sten Rönnberg et al., "Prevalence and Risks of Pathological Gambling in Sweden," *Acta Psychiatrica Scandinavica* (forthcoming); G. Bondolfi, C. Osiek, and F. Ferrero, "Prevalence Estimates

of Pathological Gambling in Switzerland," *Acta Psychiatrica Scandinavica* 101, no. 6 (2000): 473–75; Kerry Sproston, Bob Erens, and Jim Orford, *Gambling Behaviour in Britain: Results from the British Gambling Prevalence Survey* (London: National Centre for Social Research, 2000).

6. Michael B. Walker and Mark G. Dickerson, "The Prevalence of Problem and Pathological Gambling: A Critical Analysis," *Journal of Gambling Studies* 12, no. 2 (1996): 233–49.

7. Rachel A. Volberg and Steven M. Banks, "A Review of Two Measures of Pathological Gambling in the United States," *Journal of Gambling Behavior* 6, no. 2 (1990): 153–63; American Psychiatric Association, *Diagnostic and Statistical Manual of Mental Disorders, Fourth Edition* (Washington, D.C.: American Psychiatric Association, 1994).

8. Bruce P. Dohrenwend, "The Problem of Validity in Field Studies of Psychological Disorders, Revisited," in T. Tsuang Ming, Mauricio Tohen, and Gwendolyn E. P. Zahner, eds., *Textbook in Psychiatric Epidemiology* (New York: Wiley-Liss, 1995), pp. 3–20.

9. Max W. Abbott and Rachel A. Volberg, "The New Zealand National Survey of Problem and Pathological Gambling," *Journal of Gambling Studies* 12, no. 2 (1996): 143–60.

10. Randy Stinchfield, "Reliability, Validity and Classification Accuracy of the South Oaks Gambling Screen (SOGS)," paper presented at the Tenth International Conference on Gambling and Risk Taking, Montreal, May–June 1997.

11. Henry R. Lesieur, "Epidemiological Surveys of Pathological Gambling: Critique and Suggestions for Modification," *Journal of Gambling Studies* 10, no. 4 (1994): 385–98; Michael B. Walker, *The Psychology of Gambling* (Oxford: Pergamon Press, 1992).

12. Robert P. Culleton, "The Prevalence Rates of Pathological Gambling: A Look at Methods," *Journal of Gambling Behavior* 5, no. 1 (1989): 22–41; Mark G. Dickerson, "A Preliminary Exploration of a Two-Stage Methodology in the Assessment of the Extent and Degree of Gambling-Related Problems in the Australian Population," in William R. Eadington and Judy A. Cornelius, eds., *Gambling Behavior and Problem Gambling* (Reno, Nev.: Institute for the Study of Gambling and Commercial Gaming, 1993), pp. 347–63; Rachel A. Volberg, "Assessing Problem and Pathological Gambling in the General Population: A Methodological Review," in Colin S. Campbell, ed., *Gambling in Canada: The Bottom Line* (Vancouver: Simon Fraser University Press, 1994), pp. 137–46.

13. Rachel A. Volberg, *Gambling Involvement and Problem Gambling in Montana* (Helena: Montana Department of Corrections and Human Services, 1992); Rachel A. Volberg, "Prevalence Studies of Problem Gambling in the United States," *Journal of Gambling Studies* 12, no. 2 (1996): 111–28; Rachel A. Volberg and Eric Silver, *Gambling and Problem*

Gambling in North Dakota (Bismarck: North Dakota Department of Human Services, 1993).

14. Howard J. Shaffer et al., "Pathological Gambling among Adolescents: Massachusetts Gambling Screen (MAGS)," *Journal of Gambling Studies* 10, no. 4 (1994): 339–62; Susan Fisher, "Measuring Pathological Gambling in Children: The Case of Fruit Machines in the UK," *Journal of Gambling Studies* 8, no. 3 (1992): 263–85; Susan Fisher, "Measuring the Prevalence of Sector-Specific Problem Gambling: A Study of Casino Patrons," *Journal of Gambling Studies* 16, no. 1 (2000): 25–51; Ken C. Winters, Sheila M. Specker, and Randy Stinchfield, *Brief Manual for Use of the Diagnostic Interview for Gambling Severity* (Minneapolis: University of Minnesota Medical School, 1997); Renee M. Cunningham-Williams et al., "Taking Chances: Problem Gamblers and Mental Health Disorders—Results from the St. Louis Epidemiologic Catchment Area Study," *American Journal of Public Health* 88, no. 7 (1998): 1093–96; Gerstein et al., *Gambling Impact and Behavior Study,* Chapter 2.

15. The term *psychometric* refers to the theory and techniques of measuring the performance of psychological tests.

16. Rönnberg et al., *Gambling and Problem Gambling in Sweden,* pp. 62–63; Rachel A. Volberg, *Gambling and Problem Gambling in North Dakota: A Replication Study, 1992 to 2000* (Bismarck, N.D.: Office of the Governor, 2001), pp. 36–41.

17. Maureen Kallick et al., *Survey of American Gambling Attitudes and Behavior,* final report to the Commission on the Review of the National Policy Toward Gambling (Ann Arbor, Mich.: Survey Research Center, Institute for Social Research, 1976).

18. Lawrence B. Nadler, "The Epidemiology of Pathological Gambling: Critique of Existing Research and Alternative Strategies," *Journal of Gambling Behavior* 1, no. 1 (1985): 35–50.

19. Public Law 104-169, National Gambling Impact Study Commission Act—August 3, 1996, sec. 2, para. 5.

20. Gerstein et al., *Gambling Impact and Behavior Study.*

21. Howard J. Shaffer, Matthew N. Hall, and Joni Vander Bilt, "Estimating the Prevalence of Disordered Gambling Behavior in the United States and Canada: A Research Synthesis," *American Journal of Public Health* 89, no. 9 (1999): 1369–76.

22. Before 1991, studies using the South Oaks Gambling Screen yielded only lifetime estimates of problem and probable pathological gambling. Beginning with the baseline survey in New Zealand in 1991, most SOGS-based surveys have yielded current estimates as well.

23. Rachel A. Volberg, *Gambling and Problem Gambling in Iowa: A Replication Survey* (Des Moines: Iowa Department of Human Services, 1995); Rachel A. Volberg, *Gambling and Problem Gambling in New York:*

A 10-Year Replication Survey, 1986 to 1996 (Albany: New York Council on Problem Gambling, 1996); Christian Jacques et al., "Prevalence of Problem Gambling in Quebec Seven Years after the First Prevalence Study," paper presented at the Tenth International Conference on Gambling and Risk Taking, Montreal, May–June 1997.

24. A Nova Scotia survey completed in 1996 is more appropriately termed a "follow-up" study rather than a "replication" survey since the two surveys employed different methods to identify respondents as problem or probable pathological gamblers.

25. For example, the combined current prevalence of problem and probable pathological gambling among respondents in Louisiana declined from 4.8 percent to 3.9 percent. This is presented as a decline of 19 percent, calculated by dividing the difference between the two prevalence rates (–0.9 percent) by the baseline prevalence rate (4.8 percent).

26. Alberta Alcohol and Drug Abuse Commission and Wynne Resources, *Adult Gambling and Problem Gambling in Alberta, 1998* (Edmonton, Canada: Alberta Alcohol and Drug Abuse Commission, 1998); Criterion Research Corporation, *Problem Gambling Study: Final Report* (Winnipeg, Canada: Manitoba Lotteries Foundation, 1995); Baseline Market Research, *Prevalence Study Problem Gambling: Wave 2* (Fredericton, Canada: New Brunswick Department of Finance, 1996).

27. This relatively high cut-off is intended to take into account the likely "wash" in these data from sampling and nonresponse error.

28. Shaffer, Hall, and Vander Bilt, *Estimating the Prevalence of Disordered Gambling Behavior in the United States and Canada,* pp. 55–56.

29. Abbott and Volberg, *Taking the Pulse on Gambling and Problem Gambling in New Zealand;* Rönnberg et al., *Gambling and Problem Gambling in Sweden.*

30. Productivity Commission, *Australia's Gambling Industries;* Paul E. Polzin et al., "From Convenience Stores to Casinos: Gambling—Montana Style," *Montana Business Quarterly* 36, no. 4 (1998): 2–14; Rachel A. Volberg and Walton L. Moore, "Gambling and Problem Gambling in Louisiana: A Replication Study, 1995 to 1998," Appendix D, in Timothy P. Ryan and Janet F. Speyrer, *Gambling in Louisiana: A Benefit/Cost Analysis,* report to the Louisiana Gaming Control Board (New Orleans: University of New Orleans, 1999); Rachel A. Volberg, *Changes in Gambling and Problem Gambling in Oregon, 1997 to 2000,* report to the Oregon Gambling Addiction Treatment Foundation (Salem: Oregon Gambling Addiction Treatment Foundation, 2001).

31. Volberg and Moore, "Gambling and Problem Gambling in Louisiana."

32. Volberg, *Changes in Gambling and Problem Gambling in Oregon.*

33. Polzin et al., "From Convenience Stores to Casinos."

34. Rachel A. Volberg and Walton L. Moore, *Gambling and Problem Gambling in Washington State: A Replication Study, 1992 to 1998* (Olympia: Washington State Lottery, 1999).

35. Volberg, *Gambling and Problem Gambling in North Dakota.*

36. Rachel A. Volberg, Marianna T. Toce, and Dean R. Gerstein, "From Back Room to Living Room: Changing Attitudes toward Gambling," *Public Perspective* 10, no. 5 (August/September 1999): 8–13.

37. Mark Griffiths, "Gambling Technologies: Prospects for Problem Gambling," *Journal of Gambling Studies* 15, no. 3 (1999): 265–83.

38. National Gambling Impact Study Commission, *Final Report* (Washington, D.C.: U.S. Government Printing Office, 1999), p. 2-4, available at http://www.ngisc.gov.

39. Productivity Commission, *Australia's Gambling Industries.*

40. In casinos, both mechanical and electronic machines that offer gambling games are generally referred to as slot machines. In jurisdictions where gaming machines are located in what previously were nongambling venues, a variety of acronyms (EGDs, EGMs, VGMs, VLTs) are used. In this report, we follow the usage adopted by the National Gambling Impact Study Commission.

41. Valerie Lorenz, Robert Politzer, and Robert Yaffee, *Final Report on Gambling Addiction in Maryland* (Baltimore: Department of Health and Mental Hygiene, 1990); Rachel A. Volberg, *Compulsive Gambling Treatment Program Evaluation: Final Report* (Albany: New York State Office of Mental Health, 1988).

42. Max W. Abbott, Maynard Williams, and Rachel A. Volberg, *Seven Years On: A Follow-up Study of Frequent and Problem Gamblers Living in the Community* (Wellington: New Zealand Department of Internal Affairs, 1999).

43. Shaffer, Hall, and Vander Bilt, *Estimating the Prevalence of Disordered Gambling Behavior in the United States and Canada,* p. 75.

44. Shaffer, Hall, and Vander Bilt, "Estimating the Prevalence of Disordered Gambling Behavior in the United States and Canada: A Research Synthesis," p. 1373.

CHAPTER 5

1. Michael Y. Sokolove, *The Myth, Life, and Lies of Pete Rose* (New York: Simon & Schuster, 1990); David A. Kaplan, "Know When to Hold 'Em, Know When to Fold 'Em," *Newsweek,* March 15, 1993, p. 68; Associated Press, "Schlichter Ordered Back to Indiana after Arrest," *Sportsline,* May 10, 2000, available at http://www.sportsline.com.

2. American Gaming Association, "Employees, Treatment Providers, State Officials Watch Live Broadcast Kicking Off Responsible Gaming Education

Week," news release, Washington, D.C., August 7, 2000; American Gaming Association, "Responsible Gaming Center Names Executive Director, Announces $3 Million Commitment Over Next Three Years," news release, January 28, 1997, Washington, D.C., available at http://www.americangaming.org.

3. American Gaming Association, *Responsible Gaming Resource Guide, Second Edition,* Carl G. Braunlich and Marvin A. Steinberg, eds. (Washington, D.C.: American Gaming Association, 1998).

4. National Gambling Impact Study Commission, *Final Report* (Washington, D.C.: U.S. Government Printing Office, 1999), p. 4-18, available at http://www.ngisc.gov.

5. Howard J. Shaffer, Matthew N. Hall, and Joni Vander Bilt, "Estimating the Prevalence of Disordered Gambling Behavior in the United States and Canada: A Research Synthesis," *American Journal of Public Health* 89, no. 9 (1999): 1373.

6. Dean R. Gerstein et al., *Gambling Impact and Behavior Study: Report to the National Gambling Impact Study Commission* (Chicago: National Opinion Research Center, 1999), Chapters 2 and 3.

7. Basil R. Browne, "The Selective Adaptation of the Alcoholics Anonymous Program by Gamblers Anonymous," in William R. Eadington and Judy A. Cornelius, eds., *Gambling Behavior and Problem Gambling* (Reno, Nev.: Institute for the Study of Gambling and Commercial Gaming, 1993), pp. 573–94.

8. Massachusetts Council on Compulsive Gambling, *Newsletter* 12, no. 3 (Summer 2000), p. 1.

9. Loreen J. Rugle, *The Treatment of Pathological Gambling,* report prepared for the Indiana Gambling Impact Study Commission (Indianapolis: Center for Urban Policy and the Environment, Indiana University, 1999).

10. Greg Jefferson, "Investors Gamble on Centers: Treating Addiction Is Duo's Goal," *Indianapolis Business Journal* (June 1998), available at http://www.ibj.com.

11. Trimeridian homepage, http://www.trimeridian.com.

12. Alex P. Blaszczynski and Neil McConaghy, "A Two to Nine Year Treatment Follow-up Study of Pathological Gambling," in Eadington and Cornelius, *Gambling Behavior and Problem Gambling,* pp. 215–34; Michael B. Walker, "Treatment Strategies for Problem Gambling: A Review of Effectiveness," in Eadington and Cornelius, *Gambling Behavior and Problem Gambling,* pp. 533–66.

13. Rugle, *The Treatment of Pathological Gambling,* p. 21.

14. Julian I. Taber et al., "Follow-Up of Pathological Gamblers after Treatment," *American Journal of Psychiatry* 144 (1987): 757–61.

15. Sheldon Blackman et al., "The Gamblers Treatment Clinic of St. Vincent's North Richmond Community Mental Health Center:

Characteristics of the Clients and Outcome of Treatment," *International Journal of the Addictions* 24 (1989): 29–37.

16. Rachel A. Volberg, *Compulsive Gambling Treatment Program Evaluation: Final Report* (Albany: New York State Office of Mental Health, 1988).

17. Randy Stinchfield and Ken C. Winters, *Treatment Effectiveness of Six State-Supported Compulsive Gambling Treatment Programs in Minnesota, Fourth and Final Report*, report to the Minnesota Department of Human Services (Minneapolis: University of Minnesota Medical School, 1996).

18. Rugle, *The Treatment of Pathological Gambling*, pp. 27–28.

19. Rachel A. Volberg and Henry J. Steadman, "Accurately Depicting Pathological Gamblers: Policy and Treatment Implications," *Journal of Gambling Studies* 8, no. 4 (1992): 401–12.

20. Max W. Abbott, Maynard Williams, and Rachel A. Volberg, *Seven Years On: A Follow-up Study of Frequent and Problem Gamblers Living in the Community* (Wellington: New Zealand Department of Internal Affairs, 1999).

21. National Gambling Impact Study Commission, *Final Report*, p. 1-1.

22. Robert P. Culleton, *A Survey of Pathological Gamblers in the State of Ohio* (Philadelphia: Transition Planning Associates, 1985); Ira Sommers, "Pathological Gambling: Estimating Prevalence and Group Characteristics," *International Journal of the Addictions* 23 (1988): 477–90.

23. Rachel A. Volberg and Henry J. Steadman, "Refining Prevalence Estimates of Pathological Gambling," *American Journal of Psychiatry* 145 (1988): 502–505.

24. Rachel A. Volberg, "The Prevalence and Demographics of Pathological Gamblers: Implications for Public Health," *American Journal of Public Health* 84, no. 2 (1994): 237–41.

25. American Gaming Association, "Responsible Gaming Center Names Executive Director."

26. National Center for Responsible Gaming, *1999 Annual Report*, available at http://www.ncrg.org/AR/annualreport.htm.

27. National Center for Responsible Gaming, "What's New: The Institute for Research on Pathological Gambling and Related Disorders," available at http://www.ncrg.org/WhatsNew/whatsnew.htm.

28. National Gambling Impact Study Commission, *Final Report*, p. 8-1.

29. Department of Health and Human Services, "Computer Retrieval of Information on Scientific Projects (CRISP)," available at http://www-commons.cit.nih.gov/crisp.

30. *1998 National Survey of Problem Gambling Programs: Report to the National Gambling Impact Study Commission* (Washington, D.C.: National Council on Problem Gambling, 1999).

31. Jason Azmier and Garry Smith, *The State of Gambling in Canada: An Interprovincial Roadmap of Gambling and Its Impact*, publication #9808,

version 1.1 (Calgary: Canada West Foundation, 1998), available at http://www.cwf.ca.

32. Productivity Commission, *Australia's Gambling Industries* (Canberra, Australia: AusInfo, 1999).

33. National Research Council, *Pathological Gambling: A Critical Review* (Washington, D.C.: National Academy Press, 1999).

CHAPTER 6

1. National Gambling Impact Study Commission, *Final Report* (Washington, D.C.: U.S. Government Printing Office, 1999), pp. 1-4–1-6.

2. Eugene M. Christiansen, "An Overview of Gambling in the United States," testimony before the National Gambling Impact Study Commission, Virginia Beach, Va., February 8, 1999; William R. Eadington, "The Economics of Casino Gambling," *Journal of Economic Perspectives* 13, no. 3 (Summer 1999): 173–92. See also Jonathan B. Taylor, Matthew B. Krepps, and Patrick Wang, "The National Evidence on the Socioeconomic Impacts of American Indian Gaming," *American Behavioral Scientist* (forthcoming).

3. Sebastian Sinclair and Rachel A. Volberg, "Submission to the U.K. Gambling Review Body on Internet Gambling," U.K. Gambling Review Body, London, 2000.

4. David A. Korn and Howard J. Shaffer, "Gambling and the Health of the Public: Adopting a Public Health Perspective," *Journal of Gambling Studies* 15, no. 4 (1999): 289–365.

5. Rachel A. Volberg, Donald C. Reitzes, and Jacqueline Boles, "Exploring the Links between Gambling, Problem Gambling and Self-Esteem," *Deviant Behavior* 18 (1997): 321–42.

6. Eadington, "The Economics of Casino Gambling."

7. National Gambling Impact Study Commission, *Final Report*, Chapter 1.

8. Robert Goodman, *The Luck Business: The Devastating Consequences and Broken Promises of America's Gambling Explosion* (New York: Free Press, 1995); John Warren Kindt, "The Economic Impacts of Legalized Gambling Activities," *Drake Law Review* 43, no. 1 (1994): 51–94; Earl L. Grinols and John D. Omorov, "Development or Dreamfield Delusions? Assessing Casino Gambling's Costs and Benefits," *Journal of Law and Commerce* 16 (1996): 49–87.

9. Edward Behr, *Prohibition: Thirteen Years that Changed America* (New York: Little, Brown and Company, 1996).

10. National Council on Alcoholism and Drug Dependence, *Significant Events in the Field of Alcoholism and Other Drug Addictions*, available at http://www.ncadd.org.history.

11. The Century Council homepage, http://www.centurycouncil.org.

12. Richard Kluger, *Ashes to Ashes: America's Hundred-Year Cigarette War, the Public Health and the Unabashed Triumph of Philip Morris* (New York: Vintage Books, 1997).

13. I. Nelson Rose, *Gambling and the Law* (Hollywood: Gambling Times Incorporated, 1986).

14. National Gambling Impact Study Commission, *Final Report*, p. 1-4.

15. Rose, *Gambling and the Law*, p. 210.

16. Ibid.

17. In January 2001, in response to questions from Congress, the Department of Defense contracted with a major management consulting firm, PricewaterhouseCoopers, to conduct a study of the impact of slot machines on overseas military installations.

18. Robert M. Bray et al., *1998 Department of Defense Survey of Health Related Behaviors among Military Personnel* (Alexandria, Va.: Defense Technical Information Center, 1998).

19. Karen Jowers, "Military Clinic Reaches Out to Those in Gambling's Grip," *Army Times*, September 4, 2000, p. 22; Associated Press, "Military Criticized as Aiding Gambling," *Washington Post*, January 16, 2001, p. 8.

20. The Internet Gambling Prohibition Act would amend the Wire Act to generally prohibit gambling through "all communication facilities." After failing to move beyond committee votes in the House and Senate in 1997 and 1998, the bill was revised in 1999 to include protection for telephone companies and Internet service providers (ISPs) and to exempt state lotteries, pari-mutuel racing, and sports fantasy leagues from the bill's sanctions. As of this writing, neither of the year 2000 versions of this bill, Senate or House, has moved out of committee.

21. Interactive Gaming News, "New Jersey Assemblymen Launch Campaign to Legalize Online Gambling," January 31, 2001, available at http://www.igamingnews.com; Interactive Gaming News, "Go Time in Nevada," March 7, 2001, available at http://www.igamingnews.com.

22. Goodman, *The Luck Business*.

23. David A. Korn, "Expansion of Gambling in Canada: Implications for Health and Social Policy," *Canadian Medical Association Journal* 163, n o. 1 (2000): 61–64.

24. National Gambling Impact Study Commission, *Final Report*, p. 8-5.

25. Max W. Abbott and Rachel A. Volberg, *Taking the Pulse on Gambling and Problem Gambling in New Zealand: Phase One of the 1999 National Prevalence Survey* (Wellington: New Zealand Department of Internal Affairs, 2000).

26. Rachel A. Volberg, *Changes in Gambling and Problem Gambling in Oregon: Results from a Replication Study, 1997 to 2000* (Salem: Oregon Gambling Addiction Treatment Foundation, 2001).

27. Max W. Abbott and Rachel A. Volberg, *Gambling and Problem Gambling in the Community: An International Overview and Critique* (Wellington: New Zealand Department of Internal Affairs, 1999).

28. Rachel A. Volberg, "The Prevalence and Demographics of Pathological Gamblers: Implications for Public Health," *American Journal of Public Health* 84, no. 2 (1994): 237.

29. Korn and Shaffer, "Gambling and the Health of the Public."

INDEX

Note: Page references followed by the letters *f, t,* and *n* indicate figures, tables, and end notes, respectively.

ABOUT THE AUTHOR

Rachel A. Volberg is president of Gemini Research, the only orga-nization internationally that specializes in managing studies of gambling and problem gambling in the general population. She holds appointments as adjunct associate professor at the School of Public Health at the University of Massachusetts, Amherst, and as senior research scientist at the National Opinion Research Center. She sits on the board of directors of the National Council on Problem Gambling and currently serves on the council's executive committee. Volberg has directed or consulted on numerous surveys of gambling and prob-lem gambling among adults and adolescents in the United States and Canada. Internationally, She has directed or consulted on gambling studies in countries as diverse as Australia, New Zealand, Norway, and Sweden. Her publications include numerous government reports, book chapters, and scholarly articles.